IT'S IN TRANSIT

It's In Transit

ANOTHER GREAT BOOK BY AWARD-WINNING
AUTHOR, DR. CHRISTINE TOPJIAN

Authors Get Published

CONTENTS

IT'S IN TRANSIT: WHAT HAPPENS WHEN WE PRAY - ix
COPYRIGHT INFORMATION - xi
RELEVANT SCRIPTURE - xiii
DEDICATIONS - xv
INTRODUCTION - xvii

~ 1 ~
God Is Always Good
1

~ 2 ~
Praying and Working
18

~ 3 ~
You Have Prayed. Now What?
25

~ 4 ~
Why We Don't Need To Pray Out Loud
35

~ 5 ~
Setting Up For Success
39

~ 6 ~
Using the Time to Change Us
53

~ 7 ~
Dead or Alive
56

~ 8 ~
Yes, You Are Worthy
68

~ 9 ~
If God Is Making You Wait, Expect More Than You Asked For
73

~ 10 ~
The Power of One & The Power of Solidarity
79

~ 11 ~
Praying According to God's Will
83

~ 12 ~
Taking Action According to God's Will
91

~ 13 ~
Intercession
101

Contents ~ vii

~ 14 ~
Worshiping God
109

~ 15 ~
Prayer Manifested...Pay Attention!
118

APPENDIX - THE POWER OF PRAYER - 123
DON'T FORGET...GRATITUDE - 127
NOTES - 133
ABOUT THE AUTHOR - 141

IT'S IN TRANSIT: WHAT HAPPENS WHEN WE PRAY

COPYRIGHT INFORMATION

Published by Authors Get Published
www.authorsgetpublished.com

Toronto, ON

Copyright © 2022 by Dr. Christine Topjian

All rights reserved. No part of this publication may be reproduced, distributed, or transmitted in any form or by any means, including photocopying, recording, or other electronic or mechanical methods, without the prior written permission of the publisher, except in the case of brief quotations embodied in critical reviews and certain other noncommercial uses permitted by copyright law.

RELEVANT SCRIPTURE

1 Thessalonians 5:16-18

16 Rejoice always,
17 pray without ceasing,
18 give thanks in all circumstances;
for this is the will of God in Christ Jesus for you.

DEDICATIONS

I would like to dedicate this book to my grandparents who are no longer with us: Grandpa Haig

(whom I never had the pleasure of meeting), Grandpa Dickran, Grandma Chake, Grandma Angele,

Great-Grandma Medz.

I believe you are all with God watching over us.

Much love. ♥

INTRODUCTION

Introduction

Why Do We Pray?

We pray because we want something good (at least, good and positive in our viewpoint) to happen. We pray to bring more joy, happiness, prosperity and positivity into our lives. We pray in faith that something that we feel will be good and pleasing and helpful to us will enter our lives. We pray because we have hope.

But sometimes, when we pray, things don't always turn around and get better as quickly as we would like. Or good things that we perceive as being good don't happen yet. Things can take a long time to get better, leaving us to wonder "Um, hello God...what is going on??? Why is this taking so long?!?" This time of not having acquired what we wish for can be a bit of a hard time and can make us question and wonder why God seems to be silent or not answering.

Prayer is a tool that God has given us as a means to access His goodness and His provision, and to ask Him for the things that we desire. Everyone has things on their hearts and that's fantastic. It is part of what makes us human and part of what makes us, well, us.

Sometimes having your prayer answered in the way that you wish it to be can take some time. We don't (as humans) always like that. Humans (generally speaking) look for and enjoy instant gratification or fairly quick gratification. I know I do. So when the thing that we are praying for takes some time, we may not like it.

This book is about what is happening in the spirit realm from the moment we make that prayer to the moment we receive what we have asked for. Something is causing the realization of our prayer to take time, so....what is that?

Where is the realization of my prayer during the times that I am waiting? I like to use the phrase: it is in transit to refer to that waiting period.

> **Hebrews 11:1** - Now **faith** is confidence in what we hope for and assurance about what we do not see.

~ 1 ~

GOD IS ALWAYS GOOD

God is always good, just as the title suggests. It is really important for us to understand this because some people make the assumption that God is distant, silent, uncaring or worse. They may assume that just because you have not seen or experienced the realization or manifestation of the prayer yet, that God isn't there, that perhaps He isn't listening, that He may be indifferent or that He does not care.

> Let me be clear: God loves you and hears and answers all prayers.

Let me be clear: no matter where you have been, what you have done, how many errors or mistakes you have made, God loves you and hears and answers all prayers. I would also like to let you know that He loves us with such a great love, that

He only wants the best of things to happen to and for us. That means that He can sometimes shield us from certain things and that's great when He does because very simply, He knows what is best for us and what isn't good for us.

For any prayer, there are three possible answers God gives to any prayer:

- Yes, and here it is
- Yes, but not right now (you will need to wait)
- No, and here is something else that is better

It is so very important to realize that God does answer all prayers. He will answer them in His timing and in His way. We need to do our best to be tuned-in to what He says, how He says it and what (if any) specific instructions and directions are included.

Tuned In To What He Says

God will sometimes give you directions and instructions that must be followed and completed before something will come to pass. This is referred to as "your part". These things need to be done because, as you may or may not know, if you don't do your part, the thing desired will not be achieved.

For example, if you have prayed for a job or for work, this is a reminder that you will need to be mindful of thoughts, feelings, and sensations that come to you in an effort to ensure that you are doing what you need to be doing for the prayer to come to pass. Life with God is a partnership - you have a part to play and so does He. If you are asking for a job but are not taking the steps required that He guides you to take to secure that job, then you are not doing your part.

How does God speak to us? He speaks to us through the Holy Spirit and it is the Holy Spirit that speaks to us, guides us and nudges us to specific things. For example, if you (further to the situation I provided further up) have prayed for a job and then God brings you a new professional contact who tells you that they have a job you would be perfect for,

How He Says It

God can speak to us in a few different ways:

- Sensations we receive
- Nudging
- Audible voice coming through spontaneous words and thoughts in your mind
- Signs and wonders
- Godly people speaking to you about something
- Opportunities that come up
- Open doors
- Scripture
- Devotionals
- Messages from proven Bible pastors
- Messages from proven church clergy
- Next steps or an open door provided from bible schools and seminary colleges

This piece of teaching was provided to me many years ago and upon observations and experiences in my life and in the lives of others around me, I know and can see just how true it is: God speaks, leads, shows and guides in a whisper so we need to be close enough to Him to hear the whisper.

God is calm and does not like to yell or scream. He speaks in a gentle, subtle, loving and caring voice. As such, when He is speaking to you, if you are not tuned into what He is saying, you are going to miss out on His instructions (and you definitely don't want that).

What Specific Instructions Are Included

This goes hand-in-hand with the last point. God is giving you specific instructions. Please pay attention to those instructions so that you don't miss out on His best.

For example, if you sense that God is telling you to go to a certain social function, but you don't know anyone there, and so you may be hesitating to go...go anyway. You may just end up meeting the love of your life there.

If He tells you to apply for a certain job but you're thinking "I already have a job", apply anyway. He sees things that you don't so He may be trying to tell you something.

If He tells you to take that course but you're thinking "Why? I already have a great career," take the course. You don't know why He is leading you to take that and trust me when I say that when He guides you to it, He has a very good reason.

One of the things I want to make clear here is that God does not always do things in the ways that you will think to do them. He can and will guide you to things that may not make a lot of sense to begin with, but He has a very good reason for guiding you to it and He knows exactly what needs to happen for a goal or an end to be accomplished.

So I say: please trust Him!

Now, for some people who may not know God well or may be a little newer to prayer and to relationship with Him, I can understand if you are nervous or a little bit skeptical. I get it. I will say here that giving it a shot (and by it I mean give your relationship with Him) a shot. There is only one real way to learn: try it.

If You Don't Pray....

Simply put, if you don't pray, you don't get. I will repeat that: if you don't pray, you don't get or you could get the wrong thing. I hope that doesn't sound too harsh but it is the truth. God responds when we take the time to pray and when we take the time to communicate with Him about our goals, dreams, wishes and desires.

If you are not taking the time to ask for something, then you are unlikely to receive it. God has provided this wonderful provision of prayer to access His heart and to ask Him to cause the manifestation of things you, your friends, your family members, etc., desire and things that are in your hearts. As long as your prayer lines up with His word, He will be working to communicate with you about it and bring it to come to pass.

Prayers Must Line Up With His Word

I cannot stress the importance of this point enough: prayers must line up with His word. Scripture. Must. God does not condone many things that may be running through the hearts of man or woman. God believes in love and He is always good so any prayer that you wish to have fulfilled must line up with His word and with His values.

He will never condone something that is outside of His will and if you are not sure about what He condones, I invite you to pick up the Bible and to read through it, seeing and understanding how good God is and what lines up with His values.

Without reading the Bible, it is difficult to know God. It is difficult to understand who He is, what He stands for, what He blesses and what He punishes. God loves all of His children and so if someone has ill-will in their heart toward another, God will deal with that in a very specific way.

Prayer: A Two-Way Conversation

Prayer was always meant to be a two-way communication channel between us and God. This means that we are supposed to also listen carefully and sense how we are being guided by the indwelling Holy Spirit. A friend of mine explained it perfectly: when you pray, an idea, a thought, a person, a resource may pop into your mind. That is God guiding you. That is God showing you how you are supposed to move forward and it helps you realize the steps that are needed to accomplish something.

If we don't pray, we are not moving things forward in terms of accomplishing them with God. Of course, you can work on things on your own, but not praying means that you will not have God's power helping you with it! I don't know about you but I think it would be very helpful to have God's power helping me in every situation in my life.

Having Faith & The Proverbial Staircase

Having faith means that while you don't see the physical evidence of your prayer answered at the moment but you believe that God is working on it on your behalf. Having faith means that you believe that God is powerful enough and good enough that He will or He is working on the realization of this for you or for the people whom it concerns. Having faith also means that you believe that God is good and that He cares enough about you to help you through something.

When we ask God for help, He will often show us just the first step. He is asking us to trust Him enough to take the first step and then, once that is done, He will show us more. In all of my experiences with Him and with prayer, I know that He always waits for me to complete the first step before He gives me any more information. Don't take that first step, He won't reveal the second.

In my first published book, Jesus Loves You, I talk about how Jesus loves you (each and every single person ever created, including those yet unborn), knows everything about you and how His help is just a prayer away. He is there, ready and available to help us out in any situation. We need only just ask.

That's a big part of Jesus' love for us: the desire (yes, that's right, He longs to help each of us) to help you through anything, big or small, tiny or massive.

"Christine, how am I supposed to ask Him for help?"

I have been asked this question many times so if you are wondering about this, know that you are not alone. Asking God for help can come in any way and at any time. We can ask while sitting in our bathtub at home, at our desk at work, while jogging on the treadmill, while feeding the baby, while picking up the kids from school, while taking a shower, while making dinner, while doing the chores, while relaxing and putting your feet up with a glass of wine at the end of the day. It doesn't matter - just ask!

Many people I have spoken to ask me two specific things about how to pray:

1. Does it need to be done in a formal way? The answer is no. We can come to God and ask Him for His help in the most simple, informal ways.

2. Can we just say anything? You are free to speak your mind but be mindful of the words we use because if you don't ask for specifics, you are not going to receive specifics.

Matthew 7:7 "Ask and it will be given to you; seek and you will find; knock and the door will be opened to you.

For example, if you are looking for a new job and you simply say *"Lord, please bring me a new job"* then you are asking Him to help bring you a job, any job. If what you want is any job, then great, you have prayed correctly.

But if you want a specific job with specific qualities, benefits, salary and givens, you have to include all of those in your request. In other words, be specific about the particulars. Be specific about the contextual parts of it. Be specific about all aspects of it so that God can bring you specifically what you desire. Now, let's pray that prayer from further above just a little differently: *"Lord, please bring me a new career in your perfect timing, one that allows me to be home with my kids when they get home from school, one that allows me to travel extensively to beautiful and exotic places, and one that allows me to have excellent health and dental benefits for my family. Bring me a new career that allows me the financial abundance of being paid very handsomely, so much so that we are able to easily pay off our remaining mortgage and one where I* can take transit to get to work each day so that I don't have to worry about transport to work every day. In Jesus' name. Amen." Now that is a very different prayer.

The Lord has granted everyone free will, which means that you have the ability to ask for anything you want and to take any action you desire. Keep in mind, though, that if you are asking for things that are not Scriptural, that there are consequences to that prayer. For example, if you ask for a million dollars and then ask God to help you rob a bank, know that He will not grant that request and doing so will land you in jail.

God listens to each word you say, each word you pray and He respects the words you select in your prayer. As such, we need to be mindful of the words we are using when we are praying. If you are someone who is unsure what words to use during your prayer, that is no problem. Ask the Holy Spirit for some help. Ask Him to bring to your mind the right words, sentences, phrases and ideas that will propel you to what He knows is really in your heart.

To illustrate that last point: Mary was having a hard time with the exact words she wanted to pray in order to get the position she knew she wanted. She decided that instead of racking her brain on this, she would leave it to the Holy Spirit. Amazingly, she received an email providing her with new information about her chosen career, allowing her vocabulary to triple in one swift shot. She now had a greater sense of the words she wanted to use in bringing about this new career. She began to use the new words she had at her disposal.

James did the same. He prayed for the Lord to give him the right words to say. A few weeks later, James found himself in an information meeting with a higher-up at the company his cousin works for and was able to ask this gentleman all kinds of questions about the company and the industry in general. He used this information to make his application and subsequent interview responses much more solid and was selected for a job at the company.

God is incredibly pragmatic. He will bring about circumstances, people, situations and conversations that you could not have made happen on your own.

God is incredibly pragmatic. He will bring about circumstances, people, situations and conversations that you could not have made happen on your own. He will line up the right people, the right connections, the most direct way to achieve the goals. Remember that there will always be a part of any context that is in your control and a part that won't be. You can put together the best application and do a great job in all the areas that are within your control....and that's great. But there will always be parts that are outside of your control and that need to be managed by God. So, you just need to ask and then you need to step back and trust Him.

So, here are some ways you can ask Him:

- Asking Him for help in your mind (for example, asking a question such as this in your mind: "God, I need Your help, You know everything that I am dealing with. I need You to give me wisdom, help, guidance, strength and so much more!")
- Praying out loud with your mouth for help
- Praying in silence with your mouth for help
- Asking friends and family to pray with you and for you
- Asking Him to line up things in your life with providential opportunities
- Talking to Him about the problems, asking Him to illuminate your mind with wonderful solutions
- Pray in tongues

When we say to step back and trust Him, it means that in that time frame, you need to be staying in faith and trusting that He will bring something to come to pass. Until you receive word of your next step, that is the step that you should be on, waiting patiently to see if you will receive next steps about anything. This waiting is very different from waiting and doing nothing. Waiting in faith is waiting for God to communicate the next steps because the process has been started; whereas waiting and doing nothing means that nothing is in motion and that, frankly, you are just wasting time.

How Can I Say That God Is Always Good?

When we see the terrible things happening in the world, we can sometimes (or often) wonder: "Where are You, God?" "Why are You allowing such terrible things to happen in the world?" While the answer may not seem simple, there is some simplicity to it and say this respectfully, reader. We don't listen.

I know for a very long time, I did not.

> The fact is: God is always speaking, warning, guiding, helping, nurturing....but are we listening? Are we obeying Him?

Here is a parallel, a "for instance" if you will: when you were or are young and your parent(s) or guardian tells you not to touch the hot stove because you will be burned, and you still do it because you were curious, because you wanted to disobey, because you just felt like it, the fact is you will be burned and it will hurt. It's the same concept with Father God: God is always speaking, warning, guiding, helping, nurturing....but are we listening? Are we obeying?

Truthfully, some do. Many don't and it may not be because you are trying to defy or you are trying to not obey, it could be because you are not close enough to hear Him and to hear His warnings.

Ask yourself these questions:

- Are we paying attention to the things He is calling to our attention?

- Are we paying attention to the things He is telling us to be aware of or to be wary of?
- Are we asking Him and following through on the things that need and require attention? If we don't heed His warnings, respectfully said, we have ourselves to blame. If we don't silence our minds and our hearts and listen to Him, His warnings, His guidance and more, then we are not heeding the Teacher's warnings and we are doing as we please. He is speaking....are we listening?
- Are we praying for His best for our lives?
- Are we listening to His commandments of "thou shall not steal?" "thou shall not covet thy neighbor's wife?" and so on

It takes practice and trust to listen to Him and to do as He guides. Does listening to Him mean that we may sometimes be a little bit uncomfortable in order to accomplish something that He has guided us to? Of course! But then again, everything good takes some time and while it may be hard to accomplish, if He has guided you to do it, it is going to be worth it.

Here is an example: A lady I know named Roda (name changed) married a very nice man. They had a lovely wedding, and they traveled the world for their honeymoon. They were happy and bought a beautiful house to live in. Things were great. Until some cracks began appearing in the marriage, and Roda shared with me that she had a choice - she could either work on these cracks and stay married to this wonderful man or she could walk away and divorce him. I suggested to Roda that she pray about this situation, as I knew Roda was a Christian. She agreed to pray about it and a short while later, she came back and advised that she sensed that the Lord was telling her that she had married the right man and that she needed to work on the difficulties and to stay married. Roda understood that but she decided to go her own way. She decided to let the marriage go (despite my encouragement to stay with him and to work things out, as was the guidance) and she filed for divorce. Fast forward to a time later and Roda expressed how truly unhappy she was with her decision to let her ex husband go but that he had now moved on so she felt that she should do the same.

The guidance was clear: Roda was to stay married to him and to work on their marriage (as all marriages need work) but she chose her own way and (very unfortunately) did suffer as a result.

My point: God is there to speak to us and guide us. Are we listening? Are we obeying? Do we have enough respect for His word to listen and to obey Him?

God is always there, loving, kind and available. He always (without exception) wants the best for us and always wants to give us His best. That is why sometimes when we strive for something that is less than His best for you, He will not give it to you because His plan is to bring you something better.

I cannot tell you how many times I have watched friends, family and colleagues pray for one thing, not get that thing but a little while later, get something much better instead. Sometimes we don't pray high enough, deeply enough...and so when we get something better, that is God's way of showing out and saying "this is how much I love you and how much I wanted to bring this fantastic thing to you!"

God Is Sovereign, God Is Good

Sovereign means to possess ultimate ruling power based on knowing the past, the present and the future. Good means that He always wants the best for others. God possesses both qualities. They are both inherent to His personality and they are both parts of Him that are intrinsic to Him. He is not only sovereign but He is also good and He wants the best for us, each and every single time.

Sometimes, when things don't make a lot of sense, we have to remember that we may not be seeing the full picture of what He is doing and what He wants for us. In Proverbs 3:5-6, it says *"Trust in the Lord with all thine heart; and* **lean not unto thine own understanding***. In all thy ways acknowledge Him, and He shall direct thy paths."* When we let the Lord direct our paths, we may be surprised at the directions in which He takes us but we have to remember that He is taking us via His route and in His timing, in His way, not our own.

Here is an example: A man I heard of named Ronald (name changed again, of course) wanted to marry Pixie. He felt so sure that she was it for him and he knew he was ready for the "wife and kids" package. He did not pray to the Lord about whether Pixie was the right woman for him and as such, he was relying on his own heart, his own mind and his own understanding. He did ask some friends and family if they liked Pixie and if they felt she was a good match for him but he failed to ask the Most High God. Had he done so, the Lord could have shown him that Pixie was actually lying to him and that she had been married twice before and was looking to take Ronald for his money. Unfortunately, Ronald did marry her and that is exactly what happened, leaving Ronald quite unhappy and soured from the whole idea of marriage.

> We always need to take the problem, question, issue or subject to God before we take it to anyone else!

We always need to take the problem, question, issue or subject to God before we take it to anyone else! If we don't, we are missing out on His best, His advice, His input and His wisdom. Don't rely on your own understanding. Rely on His.

~ 2 ~

PRAYING AND WORKING

This is a very important topic, so I knew that it needed a chapter all on its own.

> We are supposed to be working in tandem and in partnership with the Lord, not on our own. As such, we need to have our actions and our prayers guided and led by Him.

Some people are of the frame of mind that because you have prayed, your part is done or that you have prayed and have faith therefore God is going to do everything for you. That is, respectfully, wrong thinking. We need to ensure that we are taking the strategic actions that He is guiding us to take and we need to ensure that we are following Him in 2 ways:

1. Doing things as He says (in the ways that He says)
2. Doing things in the timing in which He says

I will give the example here of a man I will name Luke. Luke was guided to start an important organization that the Lord was leading him to and began by giving him the first steps to undertake, starting off simply and easily. There were three steps to begin and I explained to Luke what those steps were and the time frame those steps would likely involve.

Luke took the first step but then mentioned that he had something important to do that weekend so he would not be able to complete the second step within the time frame allotted. I reminded Luke that the second step could easily be done online and that it would take him a maximum of about 30 minutes to do so, time that he had while he was passively waiting for a service to be completed that weekend. The time passed and Luke did not take the second step. I sent him a gentle reminder about it and then the Lord advised me that the first reminder was needed but then, I was to stop, noting that Luke knew the timeline and should have kept within them. Because of that missed timeline, Luke missed out on an important deadline, and missed out on the Lord's best (and a healthy discount he would have received if he had worked within the right timelines). Fortunately, Luke chose to repent for that error and the Lord is sure to forgive so we must always try to work within the time frames that the Lord gives us because He has a reason for having asked us to take on that task when He gives us those parameters. Again, fortunately, Luke chose to continue with the Lord's directions for the other steps and he completed those steps within the time frames given.

Working Strategically

When we work in tandem with the Lord, we can be sure and confident that we are working in the best possible ways and toward the most strategic goals. We can also be sure that we are working within the best possible contexts because God knows our time is valuable and He does not enjoy having us waste our time.

When we work without the Lord's guidance, we are not only toiling in vain but we are working without His power being released into the situation.

Here is a Scripture passage (Matthew 7:24-27) that shows this:

The Two Foundations

24 *"Therefore, everyone who listens to these messages[a] of mine and puts them into practice is like a wise man who built his house on a rock.*
25 *The rain fell, the floods came, and the winds blew and beat against that house, but it did not collapse because its foundation was on the rock.*
26 *"Everyone who keeps on hearing these messages[b] of mine and never puts them into practice is like a foolish man who built his house on sand.* **27** *The rain fell, the floods came, the winds blew and battered that house, and it collapsed—and its collapse was total."*

You Don't Have To Work On It....You Get To Work On It

We need to keep in mind that being able to work on something is a blessing. Your work is your craft and while we may not always see it as a blessing, it really is one. Think about how many people out there would love to have the skills that you may be taking for granted. Think about how many people out there would love to be able to do the things you do and in the ways that you do them. Each skill that we have is a blessing, is a gift from God, from being great at lawn care to being great at health care to being a great teacher or a great nurse to everything in between. There are no professions or jobs that are not worthy, that are not awe-inspiring. I constantly look around me and I am in awe when I see people doing great work, no matter their post, station or calling. It's amazing because while I can try my hand at something, that person may have a way of doing the task that is very different from a way that I would do it and as such, I say good for them for doing that and in the way that they do it!

I am also in awe of people who do jobs that I know I am not suited for. I was watching a health care worker recently working with my family member and her care, her patience, her work ethic and her kindness to my family member were all part and parcel of what made her such a great worker. She was great at doing a career that I would not be suited for.

So, when you do your work, remember that you get to do it. It is your privilege to do it. It is a blessing that you get to do it. And I suggest you approach each day with that frame of mind, as much as possible.

When the Lord guides you to do a task or tasks in a certain way, that is part of the "it's in transit" process. He is showing you how you are going to accomplish that thing and He shows you what needs to happen to make the blessing manifest.

Holy Spirit-Led Seeing

Let's do an exercise where we tap into the Holy Spirit and ask Him to show us a visual of the "it's in transit" process. Yes, this is meditation and it goes a long way in helping us to 1) calm ourselves   2) gain perspective   3) tap into the wonderful powers provided to us by the Lord through the indwelling Holy Spirit

So, let's begin:

1. Get to a quiet space where you are least likely to experience interruptions
2. Sit comfortably and close your eyes
3. In your mind, ask the Holy Spirit to speak into your heart and to provide you with a visual of what He wants to show you
4. Hold the image steady and ask the Spirit specifically what He wants to show you with that
5. Look carefully at all parts of the image. See all aspects of it as carefully as you can, asking the Spirit to focus in on anything specific
6. Enjoy your time doing this and let the image provided by the Spirit wash over you

This is a very effective meditation and needs to be done consistently. Meditation is a tool provided to us by God to help us get and stay calm, to see the goodness He wants to bring us and much more. Remember that this is a visual representation and the reality you experience may not look 100% the same but the idea is there.

Documenting

Documenting is the process of writing down the names, dates, images, sensations and more that you receive during your prayer time and during your meditation time. I would highly suggest documenting everything because it not only gives you a reference from which to work, but it helps keep information and dates accurate and top-of-mind.

Over time, memories can get fuzzy and it is often very helpful to write down the information we have gotten, in an effort to ensure that we have remembered things correctly, that we have gotten the information down right and that we can keep track of timelines.

You will likely look back on your journaling one day and you will get a refresher of what was said and when and how.

I often look back on my journaling and I see just how much guidance I got from God on something, how much time I put into it, how much effort and more. It is really amazing to see just how much we put into something when we look back on it with accurate detail. I also want to point out that it's great to keep a copy of these things so that if you are ever in a position to coach others in journaling and in the ways of following God, that you can look back and show them what that really looks like.

In an effort to give you some space to journal and to talk to God through the indwelling Holy Spirit, I have included some space here and some additional pages at the end of this book that you can use to journal as you make your way through this book, jotting down what you did, thoughts you had, impressions and prayers you made. Including the dates and times for each would be amazing and wise because then you can accurately know when things were written, which is great for tracking your progress.

~ 3 ~

YOU HAVE PRAYED. NOW WHAT?

Ok, so you prayed. Good. Now what happens? Do you wait? Do you move? Do you go forward? What do you do?

Know this to begin with: God hears each and every prayer, no matter who you are, where you are, what language you are speaking or whether you are saying the prayer in your mind or out loud with your mouth. He hears your prayers and He knows what is on your heart. And in addition to that, He loves you just the way you are today and is ready to answer your prayer requests.

Prayers are a request you make to God telling Him what you would like to see happen. When we use the term manifest (I have written books on manifesting), what we mean to say is that we are looking to cause something to appear in real, physical life. Here is a list of just some of the items I have watched family, friends, and loved ones pray for and asked to manifest. Of course, your list can look totally different from these and that's fine because ultimately, your prayer is your request.

Here is a list of some prayers people have prayed, seeking happiness, joy, health and prosperity in their lives and the lives of their loved ones:

- Happiness and health for you and your loved ones
- Deliverance from sickness, trials and diseases
- An increase or turnaround in financial situation
- A new job or opportunities
- To conceive and to deliver a happy and healthy baby
- For your children or tweens or teens to accept Christ
- For your children to come to church with you
- For a stronger marriage with your spouse
- For safety and security as you take a trip
- For a new car, job, or opportunity
- To be able to make rent
- To be able to fully pay off one's mortgage
- To buy one's first home
- To have your first or second, etc., pet
- For a friend or family member to have peace in their minds or in their hearts
- For accolades for a job you put tons of time and energy into
- To meet and marry or re-marry
- To be able to travel around the world
- To have great friends and confidants we can share our lives with
- To be happy
- To have a sound mind
- To have a sound body
- To be happy at work

- For a loved one to get through a surgery with tremendous success
- For a new tv or laptop or product
- For that promotion you or a loved one have been working really hard for
- For a great financial break
- To be able to see better or to see at all
- To be able to hear better or to hear at all
- To be able to walk better or to walk at all
- For more confidence

I think it is safe to say we all have at least one thing in common: we all have things we would like. It doesn't matter who you are, in what part of the world you live or what your name is, we all have things we want and part of the human condition is to have those things, people, places, circumstances, etc., you would like to appear in your life and you would like to be able to manifest.

That is the very purpose of prayer. So, I am going to now explain what happens from the moment you pray.

From the moment you pray, God starts working!

As soon as you begin to pray, God starts working. He starts to put in place all the many pieces that are required, He starts to move things around and shift things around so that He can, in His perfect timing and in His perfect way, bring us what we have asked for, if it is His will for us to have it.

You see, every prayer requires circumstances, people, and situations to be in place for its manifestation, so when you pray, He immediately starts to move things into action, move things around and makes sure that He is bringing you what you have asked for in the quickest way and in the best way.

He knows all the steps that are required to bring that dream to you. Here is an example: Joey has prayed for a promotion at work. The following are the steps that could be required to occur for the manifestation of that prayer to occur:

- The company owner decides that this position and its functions are necessary enough that they are willing to pay someone to perform them
- The company has to put the posting out to the employees and possibly to the public to advertise for candidates to apply for the position and the criteria for applications
- Joey sees the posting in time and decides to apply
- Joey's resume, education, and experience have to conform to the demands and the requirements of the position
- The manager of Human Resources has to successfully receive Joey's online application (which means the technology also has to work properly)
- Joey's application, CV and cover letter have to meet keyword requirements of the posting in order to pass through the company's tech filters

- The hiring committee of the posting has to notice Joey's application and deem his application worthy of an interview meeting
- The hiring committee of the posting needs to schedule a time and date to meet with Joey to discuss his qualifications and then contact Joey to establish the meeting date
- Joey has to be or become available at that date and time
- The technology has to work for the meeting to take place
- Joey has to show up and do his best in responding to the interview questions
- The company has to decide (post-interview) that Joey is the right person for the job
- The company has to then offer the position to Joey
- Joey has to receive the job offer and to accept the position and all the particulars of the position

This is just a sample scenario to explain to you and to give you a sense of what would be involved in this prayer and why it would take some time for the prayer to manifest and come to reality for Joey. **Many things have to line up for Joey to get offered and accept that promotion and God is behind all of it**. He is the One who is going to influence and cause everything to happen and He is always working behind the scenes to make sure that everything is falling into place as it needs to.

John 5:17 My Father is always working and so am I.

> For every single prayer that is prayed, God is working behind the scenes to set the stage and to set (and keep) in motion all that is needed for the realization of that prayer to happen.

For every single prayer that is prayed, God is working behind the scenes to set the stage and to set (and keep) in motion all that is needed for the realization of that prayer to happen.

Keep Praying, Keep Believing

Prayer is what helps the oiled machine keep moving in the right direction. When we stop praying for something, God cannot move on our behalf. He needs us to pray and to keep praying for the right things to line up for us.

Some people can easily become frustrated when they don't see things moving as they feel they should, and I get that. I have been there too. They can become frustrated, stop praying and think or say *"forget this....this sucks....I'm done with prayer"* not realizing that they may very well be close to the very manifestation of what they have asked for, they just gave up praying a little too early.

Here is a visual that I like to refer to that helps me see this concept practically:

I love this image because it shows you that you have to keep working at something, keep plugging away at it, keep focusing on the job at hand to get to where you want to be because you have already gotten things into motion and that took hard work and time for prayer. Why don't you honor your work and God's work and keep in faith, plugging away at it and continuing to pray and ask for where it is.

One of the things I want to mention here in this section is that I know how hard it can be to pray for something and to not receive it until much later, or not receive it at all. I have had the Lord tell me many times that I would not be getting something or that a person that I thought I wanted in my life was in fact not the right person to want in my life and in the beginning, I did not take it well. It actually felt devastating. At the time.

Now, I look back on it and I realize that the blessing was that I didn't get it.

> It takes a lot of trust to follow the Lord and to put down what you think you want and to go with what He says.

It takes a lot of trust to follow the Lord and to put down what you think you want and to go with what He says. It does take a lot of trust and that can be difficult for some but I practice what I preach so I can tell you that I have done it and in hindsight, I genuinely feel that His way was and is the best way. When you step back and look at all that God is guiding you to and away from, you can see a wonderful tapestry being knit - one where you get to receive certain blessings and you can see others also receiving their blessings.

I remember the first time He told me to take my hand off a certain desire. I was so sure (in my emotional state) that this was what I wanted and that I could not want anything else as much. When I finally took a step back and prayed for God to explain His plan and tapestry, I could see very clearly why He was guiding me away from that thing and how ultimately, it would not have been the right path for me. That was several years ago and I continue to look back and reaffirm that same realization today. In other words, I didn't end up changing my mind and realizing that nope, God was wrong and that thing would have been the best thing for me. I realized, in hindsight, that His way was the best way.

> God always has three possible answers.

So, I will share this little schema with you of God's three possible answers. This applies to every person no matter who you are, what you have prayed or how often you pray for something:

1. Yes, and here it is.
2. Yes, but the timing isn't right so please wait while I work on you and on others that will be instrumental to the manifestation of this blessing.
3. No, and here is something better.

If God is guiding you away from something, it is with good reason. He is not trying to be mean or trying to withhold some good thing from you. He is doing so because He is letting you know that He has prepared this for you and it is the right thing for you or the right person for you.

And this applies to every area of your life. I remember when the Lord was clearly guiding me away from a friend I had in my life. She and I had an active friendship and so I was completely confused about why He was guiding me away from her. But then I took a closer look at things. I also prayed for Him to give me the wisdom to see things through His eyes.

The picture started to look really different.

I began to notice and to see all the little put-downs, the lack of respect, the lack of good and solid moral character that she displayed, the lack of honesty in her dealings with many things, and finally, that she had introduced me to a new age group. I came to realize He knew her and me better than anyone else, and He knew who would be a good and positive influence in my life and who wouldn't. God knows the heart of each person.

When we take God's word for it, we can save ourselves a lot of heartache and headache. And sometimes we need to go through the mud to see that He was right the whole time and that we should have listened. He will always let us make our own choices, ultimately, because He has given us free will, but if we don't realize and obey that He has guided us away from something, then the negative that comes with it is our own fault. He guided us and warned us....we just didn't listen and/or obey.

Either way, He is always guiding us. Are you listening? Are you obeying?

~ 4 ~

WHY WE DON'T NEED TO PRAY OUT LOUD

We can pray out loud with our mouth or we can pray in our minds. Either way, the prayer is valid, counts and God has heard it. How so or how do I know that? Because God is Omniscient and Omnipresent. He hears our thoughts and He knows our hearts. So when you pray, you can select how you are most comfortable praying, knowing that either way, He hears it and it counts.

One of the things that is most important about prayer is not so much about praying out loud but rather, expressing yourself clearly and saying what you wish would happen. And then, try your best to listen.

Prayer was always meant to be a two-way conversation. One where you pray and then, you listen to hear what God is saying. He is going to speak to you in any way that He wants to and that you will tune in to and He is going to guide you in the ways that are best for you.

Another part of a prayer being in transit is the time it will take to hone your ability to develop being able to hear Him. How can we be led by Him if we don't tune into Him and to what He has to say?

Specific Questions

Can we ask Him specific questions about where things with your prayers stand? Of course! And you should!

This is one of the many great things about this kind of relationship with God - we can ask Him anything at any time and He loves to be asked questions. Asking Him questions about where things stand shows Him that you are relying on Him, that you are depending on Him and that you understand that He only wants the best for you.

There is no one set way to ask Him but here are some suggested questions you can ask (remember to input all the details you want to know about and then listen carefully for words, phrases, feelings you receive, etc.):

- God, where do things stand with this prayer? Would You speak to me specifically about this?
- Lord, what do You want me to know about this situation?
- Where do things stand in terms of my prayers about x, y, z?
- Lord, is there anything I am supposed to be doing now that I am not doing?

- Lord, are there delays happening in the fulfillment of my prayer and if so, can you speak to my heart about them and can you remove the things causing the delays?

When I say that our relationship with God is truly one of a loving, caring, meaningful and active relationship, I mean that. You are supposed to be able to go to Him with anything!

Private Prayers

Another reason for which we don't need to pray out loud for something is because many times, we are not alone. There could be people around us at work, at home, in a public area, etc. Many people don't want others to hear their specific prayers (and rightly so) and so oftentimes, private prayers are the best.

Private prayers are those prayers that we make in our minds and in our hearts. They are equally heard by God, in just the same way as prayers out-loud are said and we always want to make sure that we are praying for things "in Jesus' name." The reason we do this is because Jesus is the One in whom we have belief and so when we believe in Him, we are asking for things in the name that is above all other names. Everything in Heaven and on earth have been put under Jesus' authority, so when we pray in His name, know that the prayer is at its pinnacle in terms of effectiveness.

Further, when we pray out loud, darkness does hear our prayers too and that isn't something that we need or that we would want. Prayers are personal, important to us and very much between yourself and God. When we speak our prayers out loud, we are opening ourselves up for others to hear it and you may not want that.

I have been asked before "*What happens if others (whom I don't want) also hear it?*" Simple. Pray to God for protection and for Him to make your prayer private, just between you and He. He has ways to do that that you do not know about.

~ 5 ~

SETTING UP FOR SUCCESS

In order to set things up for success, some time and some attention will be needed. In this time, you need to take strategic action, pray, and allow things to begin shifting in your favor, and you will need to be working at the tasks you need to complete, and God will be working on the tasks He needs to complete. After all, putting good & worthwhile things in place takes some time. These pieces that need to be put together are all part of transit time.

> God is a God of order, of steps, of processes and of ensuring that things are done right.

God is a God of order, of steps, of processes and of ensuring that things are done right. He is not a slapstick God who throws things together, hoping that something will eventually stick. This is a very important point and when considered mindfully, will help people understand why there is a transit time to begin with. Why do we have a waiting period in the first place? Why can't we just pray for something and it just shows up immediately? No muss, no fuss.

> In the physical realm, things take some time, so when we pray spiritually for something, it is now formed. It just takes some time for it to be physically manifested.

Because it takes time to set things up in the physical space. We have to, with intention, create something in our minds and then work on it in the physical sense. If we want God's help, then we pray for that, asking Him to come into the situation and to help us, giving Him some time to get to work on our behalf. Now, God is in control of everything so some may ask "Why does He make us wait? Why can't I automatically have what I want right now?" Simple. Waiting provides time for all of the following to occur:

- Time for you to learn to be patient
- An opportunity for you to trust that He is working on it, even when you don't yet see it
- Time for God to work, to move and to shift things around
- Time for Him to influence the right people and cause the right circumstances to come into place
- An opportunity for you to get close to Him and to build on your own personal relationship with Him while waiting in faith

- An opportunity for you to pray about where things are, allowing you to grow in your relationship with Him
- Time for ideas to form in key peoples' minds, for documents to be drawn up or changed, for new people, circumstances and situations to come into play

The following will provide an illustration of what working with God is like (and what can happen during the transit time) versus what working without God is like:

Working with God: Say you want a new job because you feel God is leading you in that direction, so you

1. Have the intention to go out and look for a new job.
2. You can pray and ask the Holy Spirit if you should go online, or how you would look for that new position - God could be leading you to go online and look, to speak to family and friends, to put feelers out, etc.
3. You can then fix up your cover letter and CV, and you can begin sending out your documents to postings that best match what you are looking for.
4. Thanking God for bringing you the offer of employment before you even get it and asking the Holy Spirit to help you see what being in that new position would look like are also great strategies to help you.

These are all steps that are part of having the intention of fulfilling what you believe God has put on your heart and then putting strategic actions behind it in an effort to move things forward.

When we pray for God's help, He can help us by doing all of the following for us: provide you with a sense of how, where and when you should go out and look for the position, He will speak to your heart about the kind of position He wills for you to have (it may be in your current industry or company and it may not), He will provide the time and space to fix up your resume (we all have busy lives so He will help free you up), He will bring the right job postings or opportunities to your attention, He will help make sure that the right people (the decision-makers or the influencers) see and consider your application above the others, and that all the pieces that are required for you to get the right position happen in the manner and in the time frame that He chooses.

Working without God: Here, you can want any new position that you want, but it may not be the right position for you, it may not lead you to the satisfaction you would be seeking in your employ, you won't have the benefit of God working things out for you and you may (unknowingly) be getting yourself into a wrong company, a wrong situation, having a terrible new work opportunity and more.

The example of Maria: Maria was a brilliant worker. She had worked for many years as a project manager, had great skills in the field and she felt tired with her current work situation so she felt she should go out and look for alternatives. She felt compelled to go look elsewhere for a new situation. She decided to do this without God. She went for her MBA (which God did not lead her to do), completed it and began job hunting. She got hired within a few weeks and she felt really happy about her new job. She began to feel really excited as she gave her notice to her current employer and let them know that she was going to be leaving. The day came and she started her new position at the new company. At first, everything seemed great - she was getting much more money, she had the flexibility of working from home, and she was in a senior level position, which basically meant that she had been promoted.

Maria felt very happy and content with her decision. On the outside at first, it seemed that even though she had done this without God's input and help, that everything was very good and that she made it happen on her own.

Then, things began to change. Her boss left the company and another director came into effect, to whom Maria would have to report and this man was condescending, terrible, unfair and rude to Maria. She then began being put down by her boss' boss, and was berated for a faux pas that had been made in a meeting but for which she was not responsible. Then, she was advised that despite the job posting having indicated that it was a fully remote position, that she would have to go in 2 times per week for the position, something that was posing a problem because Maria and her spouse did not have an extra car. Little by little this awesome position that Maria had gotten in her own strength began to unravel and Maria found herself to be utterly miserable. She knew that she needed to do something but did not know what.

One of the things that I find so amazing about the way God works is that because He knows each of us so well, He is able to perfectly gauge where we are, how we may need to change and improve, as well as what we will need to change and to improve for future growth as well. God doesn't want us to go through unnecessary hardships and that's why when He guides, He leads us to His best and to access that best through the fastest possible means.

When we go it on our own, we are taking steps of our own accord and we are functioning without His help. Why would we do that to ourselves? Why would we voluntarily put ourselves at a disadvantage when we can have the power of God working actively for us?

Yes, it takes time to set up situations, circumstances, change people's hearts, influence people and much more, but by including God and by following His ways and His path, we are allowing the power of God to float through our situation and we are working in partnership with Him. That sounds pretty good to me!

The following are some examples from my own life and from the lives of those around me, intended to demonstrate what it was that took time to set up and therefore, why the fulfillment of the prayer was in transit, versus having been quickly fulfilled and manifested.

- A lovely young lady had prayed for the right career position to come along. She was a single woman and had many expenses. She prayed to God that He would bring her the right opportunity. She believed that she was meant to work in nursing and was focusing her prayers on that. Over the next few months, the Lord began to show her that her skill set was actually more meant for the field of teaching, and that that's where God wanted her to be. She was always a praying woman but never knew that there was such a thing as inner locution where the Lord would, could and does speak to you directly to tell you His will for you. It took her several months to get this practice down very well but once she had it, she would journal each day and was able to easily discover what and where the Lord was guiding her. She was able to get a wonderful position within the field of teaching, which she was very happy with and very grateful for, and allowed her to explore a skill set that she didn't even know she had.

Had she not trusted in the Lord, she would not have taken the steps required to become a teacher and to get that teaching position.

- Mark felt that he wanted to be a bachelor for the rest of his life. He had watched his parents' marriage go down the drain and end in a very bitter divorce. As such, he had told himself that he never wanted to get married. He entertained women and enjoyed himself but refused to get tied down. The woman meant for him, Janet, was a lovely and kind praying woman who had been friends with Mark for many years. She prayed frequently and deeply for the Lord to reveal to her whom the husband she was meant to be with was (at that point not knowing that the man meant for her was Mark) and asked that the Lord show her during one of her quiet prayer times who the right man for her was. One afternoon while she was praying, Mark's name and face came to her mind. Janet was baffled. She did not understand how and why this man was for her when he was her friend and had made it clear to anyone and everyone that he had no intentions of ever settling down. When Janet took this confusion and question to the Lord, God informed that Mark needed to be changed. Janet felt a bit confused and angry that she would have to work hard to pray for God to change this man (she could not change him herself) but realized that she needed to do this and it took many months of prayers on Janet's part to change Mark and to transform him into the man he needed to be for he and Janet to have the kind of Christ-centered marriage that God intended. In the end, Mark did change but it took a serious amount of praying, faith and patience on Janet's behalf to achieve any change in him.

Remember that we cannot change a person. That is completely and exclusively God's job - Janet's prayers were only meant to get God to move and to work from the inside out within Mark and the time frame needed to change Mark was the in transit time required.

- Barb was a Canadian and had married a wonderful God-fearing man from the US. This man was sweet, kind and very loving. Barb was a praying woman and she had made the decision to follow God and to marry this man, knowing and strongly sensing that he was the one for her. Their relationship progressed beautifully and they were on the same page on most or all issues. They were both God-fearing and praying people who believed in going to church regularly and Barb truly felt that her blessing had come. The issue was that, as they decided to live in the States because his work was there, Barb had to apply for citizenship in order to live in the States. An error had been made on her husband's part on the papers, which was causing a huge load of problems and Barb was ordered to leave the States immediately. She felt devastated. Here she was a newly married woman making her home and her life with her new husband and planning for the future and then she was kicked out of the country. Barb began praying fervently. She began praying long and hard for the Lord to intervene and for the Lord to help her papers be processed quickly so that she would be able to stay and live in the States with her husband. She also asked friends, family members and clergy members at her church to pray for the situation to be resolved quickly so that she could go back to the States. Finally, months later, her papers came through and she was able to return to their home in the States. When the officer spoke to Barb, he notified her that the process would have taken much longer but that the other claims in the pile happened to resolve themselves exceptionally quickly, allowing them to get to her case sooner. He advised that the process usually takes years but in her case, only took a few months.

    Barb knew that the processing of the papers was in transit but that she also had to help things along by praying fervently....and she did.

- Rocco had been dealing with mental health issues all his life. He had felt unhappy since his breakup with his girlfriend years ago and had felt that things were not well with him. He felt sad and alone a lot, despite having lots of friends and family to be there for him, a good stable career and was an athlete. He realized that he needed some help to process what was going on because he felt he didn't have a reason to be sad and unhappy all the time. He had to figure out why he felt the way he did. On the encouragement of his friend, Rocco prayed for God's help and His insights on why he was always feeling so sad. Rocco's friend suggested he come to church with him and that being there might help to make him feel better. When the worship music started at church, Rocco felt incredible. He felt happy, elated even, and that he felt tremendously at peace. Rocco felt amazing and he was enjoying the process of singing the songs and being in worship. In conversation with his friend afterward, Rocco explained that God had answered his prayer of lifting him from the sadness and that being in church was the first time he had genuinely felt happy in years. His friend suggested that he join the church worship team, who pray and sing together regularly, and that that might be a direction God is leading him into. Rocco grabbed the opportunity and began to pray with and join the worship team. He felt God was leading him to be a worship leader at the church and approached the head pastor about it. The head pastor said that he would pray about it but that they would love to have Rocco join as a team member for the time being. Rocco jumped at the opportunity. As the weeks wore on, Rocco got more involved with the church and realized that singing songs of worship and creating new songs for widespread sharing was something he was being called to do. The Lord had used his unhappy state to signal to him that he was being called to do something greater and that this opportunity was going to open new and awesome doors for him.

It took a little bit of time (in transit) for everything to come into place and for Rocco to become lead worship leader in the church but it did happen and when he had reached that level, he could see important doors continuing to open for him.

When we trust in God and we pray, God gets to work. He wastes no time in lining up the right opportunities, the right circumstances, the right people and the right connections to get you to where you need to be, according to Him. Of course, we have free will and we can do whatever we want, but we are not free of the consequences of doing whatever we want and oftentimes, we have operated only from our own human desire, not tapping into the greater plan that God has for us.

Therefore, in an effort to get to where God wants you to be and to live your best life, check-in with Him and see where He wants you to be and where He wants you to go. All power on earth and in Heaven have been given to Him so He is very able to do exceedingly above and beyond what we can imagine.

Getting More Educated

Sometimes, God will put a dream and a goal on our heart but knowing that we do not yet have the prerequisites for its fulfillment. He will then guide you to the learning, the classes, the program, the experience that will be required to fulfill that dream.

For example, when I knew that I wanted to be a professor in a University setting, each job posting that I came across asked for a Doctorate degree. I did not, at that time, have that. So one morning, very early, I prayed about this and God led me to an online University where I could begin taking a course or two, to get a feel for the University, for the program, for the course work and more. I was not intended to get my Doctorate and did not really see that He was guiding me to that path. I simply registered for the first course and began that. I loved it and found it interesting, appealing and very relevant to my everyday life and to my walk with God. So, I then took the second course, and then the third, and then the fourth. I was making my way through the coursework fairly quickly because I had lived through much of the material being described and had already begun and had experience journaling with God, having conversations with Him and getting His guidance, take and advice on things in my life. The coursework was challenging but interesting and I did not feel overwhelmed at most points.

Before I knew it, the administrator advised me by email that I was halfway through an accredited Doctorate program. I was shocked. I was just taking courses that were interesting and would help me in my understanding and my walk. I did not realize that He was guiding me to do that for the purposes of getting a University faculty job or even more....

God does not always give you a dream that you can easily attain. When He puts something on your heart, know that it will be beyond what you currently have education-wise, money-wise, most likely status-wise, etc. He does that in an effort for you to grow, to mature, to wisen up even more and most importantly, so that you learn to depend on Him 150%. It is never meant to drown you, overwhelm you, create tons of worry for you or worse...

If He has put something that seems near-impossible on your heart, pray and ask what are the steps He would have you take toward its fulfillment. And remember, it may not make sense to you right away and that is ok. It does not have to.

What is something that He has put on your heart that may seem impossible to you? Use the space below to reflect on that and if you would like, journal about it. Remember that there is also space at the back of the book too.

~ 6 ~

USING THE TIME TO CHANGE US

There are times when God uses the time He is making you wait to change you. This means that He is trying to develop a certain level of patience in you so that you can learn to:

- Trust in Him
- Rely on Him
- Be closer to Him
- He allows you to glimpse the process it takes to achieve your desired goals
- He shows you any steps that may be causing delays
- He may be giving you an opportunity to pray through delays

I remember one time when He had me speak with someone in a chance conversation. He was trying to show me an area of attention that was needed and that I hadn't been conscious of so

I hadn't prayed over that aspect of it. A chance phone call had come from a complete stranger and it was a little nudge He was using to guide me to focus my prayers on an area I wasn't yet conscious of. Because of this chance phone call, I realized where things actually stood with a case I had been praying about and for and it helped me see where my prayers needed to be focused. This is part of the "it's in transit" time and it's part of God guiding us, our prayers and our intentions. Within that conversation, I had received critical pieces of information that I needed to know about the people involved, and that I never would have known without the information from that phone call. God has a great way of orchestrating things so that He brings us all that we need to accomplish something.

Another Example

A lady I know, Dana, was going through a bit of a hard time. Among many personal things she was dealing with that were slowly taking a toll on her, she was looking for her longtime boyfriend, Mike, to propose. She had prayed about him and she felt the Spirit was guiding her to this man. But he wasn't proposing. Dana had prayed for him to finally pop the proverbial question and finally, a chance encounter with his mom revealed a fear that he had harbored that he had never shared with Dana. His mother knew about the fear and she had a little heart-to-heart with Dana right there, in the grocery store, where Dana never usually went shopping. Dana learned about a fear her boyfriend had that was impacting him and that he had not yet told Dana about but that needed to come to light. Dana was able to approach her boyfriend about this in a kind and respectful way and they were able to deal with the issues together.

You see, readers, God will bring you circumstances, conversations, encounters, situations that will help you understand where things stand and how to move things forward. He will always honor your prayer and faith efforts by providing you with an outlet to move things forward - it just may not be in ways that you would expect so you always have to keep your eyes open and peeled. Can you pray for God to open your eyes so that you don't miss the opportunity? Of course. You can and you should. It is really important to ensure that you are staying in faith while you are praying for something because faith is the fuel that gets God to move in your favor and for your benefit.

~ 7 ~

DEAD OR ALIVE

In the Bible, we are presented with prayers from well-meaning and intentioned people who were praying for certain things to happen, namely, for loved ones to heal or to get better, some having even already died while they were waiting for Jesus to either come and visit the person or to pray for the person.

What is amazing is that God is not bound by time and the circumstances that time brings.

IN JOHN 11:38, JESUS RAISES LAZARUS FROM THE DEAD:

38 Jesus, once more deeply moved, came to the tomb. It was a cave with a stone laid across the entrance. **39** "Take away the stone," he said.

"But, Lord," said Martha, the sister of the dead man, "by this time there is a bad odor, for he has been there four days."

40 Then Jesus said, "Did I not tell you that if you believe, you will see the glory of God?"

41 So they took away the stone. Then Jesus looked up and said, "Father, I thank you that you have heard me. **42** I knew that you always hear me, but I said this for the benefit of the people standing here, that they may believe that you sent me."

43 When he had said this, Jesus called in a loud voice, "Lazarus, come out!" **44** The dead man came out, his hands and feet wrapped with strips of linen, and a cloth around his face.

Jesus said to them, *"Take off the grave clothes and let him go."*

In this example, we can see how Jesus is not bound by the circumstances He sees. He is not bound by time, death or anything. As such, even if your situation seems dire or seems like it will never turn around, take heart and have faith that Jesus is not bound by the circumstances and that He can turn anything around.

Let's say for example that something very unfortunate happened to you and that you feel that too much time has passed and that things will never get better with that. Know and take comfort in the fact that God can make anything happen, He can turn any situation around, He can fix anything and He can bring good out of any situation, no matter how much time has passed.

Further, we have to remember that God sometimes lets us go through difficulties so that He can prove Himself and His power, so that He can test your faith or so that He can show you that He does not need things to happen in the natural because He is a Supernatural God.

What do I mean by that? Take a look at these examples:

- Lianne wanted to get pregnant with her first but every doctor told her that she would be unable to have children. They told her the chances were absolutely zero and that the infertility issues that ran in her family were not going to allow her to carry her own children. But Lianne knew that she served a Supernatural God and that her God was not bound by the medical reports or by anything else. She continued to stay in peace and to stay in faith that she would, one day, deliver her baby herself. When Lianne turned 50, her family all but gave up. They said it would now be absolutely impossible and they all urged her to give up. Lianne and her husband, Don, stayed in faith knowing that God is Supernatural. At the age of 55, Lianne finally gave birth to their happy and healthy baby girl and then, as another wonderful twist of faith, she then got pregnant with their second. When Lianne and Don went for the ultrasound to check on the baby, the doctor informed them that they were going to have not one, not two but three more children.

The woman everyone said was infertile and would never bear children ended up giving birth to four happy and healthy babies that were biologically their own!

- Mark was believing for his future wife. He felt deeply that he would meet her at church and then one Sunday, he met Helen, a stunning, statuesque woman who was new to his church. Mark was very excited and she caught his eye immediately. Mark knew that he wanted to meet her but that the timing had to be right - Helen was new to the church and he didn't want to scare her off. Over the next few weeks, Mark kept his distance but kept praying for a chance encounter. Finally, one Sunday after the service, Mark was in a casual conversation with his friend and his friend said "Mark, I'd like to introduce you to Helen. She is from the States and is new here. Helen, meet Mark, he has been a church-goer here for many years and a fine gentleman." It was the chance encounter Mark had been waiting for. He shook hands with Helen and they began chatting. He asked more about her and they got into a delightful conversation. Mark's friend later told him in private that Helen had noticed Mark at the church and asked him to introduce her. You see, Helen was getting out of a bad marriage and she was looking to settle down again with someone who was a devout Christian man and would treat her the way she deserved. You see, God can use any people, events and circumstances to bring you into your destiny.

- Obenewa was a young medical student. One evening, after class, she approached her professor about a section of the curriculum she had been having trouble with and asked him for some extra help. He told her that she was expected to figure it out on her own but that if she really wanted help, she would need to "sweeten the deal for him". Obenewa was floored and appalled. All she wanted was a little help from her professor and instead, she was being propositioned. Obenewa went and reported this harassment to the head of the department, who told her that there was nothing he could do - it would be her word against his and the professor in question had long ago been tenured so his job was guaranteed for life. Obenewa was out of options in that sense but she knew she served a Supernatural God. Obenewa prayed for God to intervene and to help her. One afternoon, after class with the same professor, Obenewa was in the restroom with another student from her class. As they were both at the sinks, the other student became emotional and started sobbing. Obenewa asked her what had been going on and the girl replied that the professor had sexually harassed her on more than one occasion and that she didn't know who to turn to. Obenewa was floored. There were now two of them that had been sexually harassed by this man and Obenewa was now wondering if there were even more girls. Obenewa prayed that the Lord would reveal the truth and that she would be able to make contact with the other women who were also harassed by the professor. Sure enough, over the next two weeks, one by one the women came forward and also claimed harassment. Obenewa was floored - every time she had prayed and asked the Lord to bring the truth and a way to light, He had done so.

- Devin was in prison for grand larceny and he was angry for having to be locked up like that. He had grown up in a broken home and he had never known what a happy home life had been. His mother drank constantly and his father had never been there for him, not once. Devin had not one positive memory of his home life and so he had fallen into a life of crime to support himself and because he didn't know any better. In prison, he was provided with a Bible to read but he had never opened it. Devin figured that God had long ago abandoned him so why should he care to even read one word of the Bible. Part of their spiritual time in prison, though, was to go to mass each week and Devin was forced to participate in this. During mass, he constantly felt a warm feeling inside of him that he had never felt before and therefore had no idea why he was feeling that. It was a very strange feeling to him but he had to admit that he enjoyed the feelings of warmth that would come over him. In mass, the prison pastor would talk about Jesus and His love for all people, no matter how many mistakes or wrong turns a person may have made. The pastor talked about how much each person could rely on Jesus to get them through absolutely anything. Something in Devin was beginning to shift. He began to slowly see and realize that the mistakes and the abandonment of his parents were not a reflection of how much Jesus loved him but rather, was part of their human brokenness. The pastor would reference Bible passages and he would talk about this story and that one from Scripture. Devin found the passages interesting but admitted to himself that he had never read any of the stories because he wanted to wash his hands of God, just like he felt God had washed His hands of him. But today was different. Devin decided to open his tattered Bible and to begin reading some of the passages and when he did, he began to see the errors of man here and there. He realized that while his life had not been easy, that there were so many others from these Scriptural stories that also had made huge mistakes but that they had come back from them. They had been redeemed and had gone on to do great things with their lives. It was the breath of fresh air Devin felt had been missing from his life and the encouragement he needed to get back on his feet and to decide to do more and better with his life with one important partner in his life: God.

- Ulia enjoyed being promiscuous with different men. She enjoyed the feeling and the warmth that came from intimate encounters and she loved being able to experience this with different men, who all made her feel a different way, at least for a little while. Ulia went to bars each night and looked for the next man who would be able to give her pleasure, not fully realizing that she was not respecting herself and not giving herself a real chance for happiness. Her friend, Martin, was praying deeply for her. He saw how she was living her life and how she needed help to realize that what she was doing was not living to her best. Martin not only prayed for her himself but he also enlisted the members of his church to pray for her too, praying for her to turn from her ways. Because of her lifestyle, Ulia had been struck with sexual diseases as well, mainly because she didn't really know much about the partners she engaged with. One evening, Martin felt the deep need to pray as he had never felt it before. He wondered what had been going on with his friend but decided to follow through on the feeling, as he sensed something was afoot. Martin got down on his knees and prayed profoundly for Ulia, hoping that she would turn completely from her ways. About a week later, Martin got a call from the hospital. Ulia had been admitted due to someone having raped and beat her and a neighbour who found her that called the ambulance. One of Ulia's dates had beat and raped her and she needed urgent medical help, as she was in a coma. Martin rushed to the hospital and prayed for Ulia's full recovery. The doctors had said the chances were about 10% that she would recover and even less that she would ever have full function of her faculties again. Each day, Martin would pray for Ulia by her bedside, hoping for her full recovery. He was asking God to intervene and to work supernaturally within Ulia. Ulia woke up 6 weeks later with all of her vital signs intact. She saw her friend Martin there praying for her and she was amazed and so happy to see him there. She explained to Martin that she had met Jesus while she was in a coma and that she was ready to give her life to Christ, she was ready to turn from her previous ways. Martin was so grateful - he realized that while he had been praying and unable to reach Ulia, that Christ had been working in her while she was in the coma and that she was ready to turn her life around. Fast forward 6 months and Ulia is in a loving relationship with her fiance, and she enjoys working as a nurse practitioner, helping others the way the nurses helped her when she was in the coma.

- Rocky was cutting himself out of self-hatred. He had been abused his whole life by various family members and he was using cutting as a way to rid himself of the emotional pain, which was very significant. He was also cutting because he felt that there was no way out. He felt trapped and he didn't know who or where to turn. Until he walked by a church one night. The door was ajar and he could hear the hymn music, which he found heartwarming. He loved hearing the pastor speak loving words about Jesus and how much Jesus loves us no matter what we have been through. He decided to go into the church for a moment. Inside, he found warm, kind, caring people who invited him in from out of the cold and offered to give him a warm cup of tea. Rocky said he would love a cup and he sat for the service. It was beautiful and heartwarming. He had heard his aunt Audrey talk about Jesus before and that had resonated with him but he had never felt anything like this. The pastor was talking about how much Jesus loved each person and was there to help us through absolutely everything. He talked about how much people could benefit from coming to Jesus because we were never supposed to carry all the burdens of life ourselves. Rocky loved what he was hearing and he asked if he could come back the next night, to which the service person attending said he could come back as often as he wanted. The door would always be open. What Rocky was looking for was love, care, compassion and much more. He was amazed that he was finding exactly what he knew he needed in a church.

It is so important to turn to God when we need help, insight, strategy, prayer and much more. Turning to Him will yield fruits that you could never have imagined or made happen on your own, or in your own strength.

> As soon as we begin to pray, God begins to get to work.

Dear readers, as you may be able to see from the stories presented here, God is able to work supernaturally in your life and in the lives of those around you. We just need to pray and we need to have faith that He is working, even when we cannot see Him working. As soon as we begin to pray, God begins to get to work. He begins to work within a person in ways we will not be able to see and He begins to change and transform a person from the inside, through a personal, loving, deeply committed relationship with Him.

If you have not yet prayed for yourself or for someone else, I would encourage you to do so. If God has put a person on your heart, He is likely guiding you to pray for that person and He is cluing you into the fact that the person needs prayers and needs help. You may be the only person praying for that person and therefore, would be taking a strong hand in their salvation and in the betterment of their lives.

If we don't pray, it's really simple. Unfortunately God won't be able to work and the person will not receive the help that they need. God is a legalist - He can only get to work within a person when either that person or another person prays for them. If God has put someone on your heart today (or in the past), take the time to pray for them. It's not too late and it does make a huge difference, even if you can't immediately see it. Take the time to ask God to help make their lives better!

> If God has put someone on your heart today (or in the past), take the time to pray for them. It's not too late and it does make a huge difference, even if you can't immediately see it.

Use some of the space provided here and jot down any names that the Holy Spirit puts on your heart, for whom it may be a good time to pray.

~ 8 ~

YES, YOU ARE WORTHY

I want to make it clear in this book and in this chapter that no matter where you have been, or what you have done, you can still go to God and repent, asking for forgiveness and you can still pray for your needs and wants and desires. God loves you no matter what and He is there to hear you out. If you have sinned (and we all have), it would be wise to repent (saying sorry) and then to proceed to ask Jesus to come into your heart so that you can have a relationship with Him. Asking Him for His help and His goodness in your life is a huge part of what our own personal relationship with Him is about.

You may know that you have done much wrong in this world. God knows it all because He sees everything and He still invites you into relationship with Him. When you repent for your mistakes, He begins to work within you to change you and to transform you into a better person.

Please note that everyone (and I mean everyone) is called to be in an active, loving and personal relationship with Jesus.

Here is a Q & A that may help you by answering some frequently asked questions I receive:

1. Q: Is it possible to do so much wrong that God turns His back on us?
A: God always wants everyone to come to Him so if you repent with an honest heart, He will not turn His back on you. Everyone is called into an active, loving, personal relationship with Him. Everyone.

2. Q: What if I am in prison. Will God still want a relationship with me?
A: Completely and absolutely yes! God wants a meaningful, personal and everyday relationship
with you no matter where you have been, what you have done, how far gone you are...He still
wants a relationship with you!

3. Q: How do I repent?
A: Repenting can be simple and amazing. You can use these words: *Lord Jesus, I know I have made   many errors and I have*

done much wrong. I am so sorry. I am asking You to come into my life and be my

    Savior. I want to live my life in tandem and in partnership with You. In Jesus' name. Amen

4. Q: I have committed _____ sin. Will God still hear & answers my

    prayers?

A: He will. Repent for your errors (in your mind or out loud). God hears the prayers for each and

    every person, no matter what.

5. Q: How do you know Jesus loves me? How do you know He is there for me?

A: Jesus died on the cross at Calvary for every single person. He paid the price for the sins of

    every person and as long as you believe in Him, you are forgiven, you have salvation and He will

    come into your heart. He is calling each and every single person into a relationship with Him and

    that relationship is loving and active and personal. Personal means that He already knows

    everything about you and loves you no matter what. Not sure if that's true? Give it a try, see

    what happens. He will answer you - you need only to keep your eyes open to see how He is

    answering you.

6. Q: How do I know that my prayers are "in transit"? How do I get confirmation?

A: Really simply, ask Him. Ask Him to show you, to give you signs and indications. You will see how He responds because He will respond and He will show up.

7. Q: What if I have prayed for something for a long time but it hasn't happened yet? What do I do?

A: Excellent question and here is a great reply: pray and ask Him. Prayers are meant to be 2-way conversations - you communicate with God and He will speak back. He will give you ideas, feelings, sensations and more. That is His way of communicating with you. You need to pay attention to those and you need to see what He is saying about the status of your prayer request.

It could be that He has already answered it and you just don't know that. It could be that He is working on it and He will show you how. It could be that there is a part you need to play to get things moving with that and He will speak to you and show you what needs to be done there.

Either way, He will show you and communicate with you. Ask. Seek. And the door will be opened.

8. Q: Am I able to pray for someone else? Will those prayers be heard and answered too?

A: Absolutely! It is great when we pray for others who may not be able to or willing to for a time.

Friends can pray with and for friends, family members, total strangers, etc. God hears all prayers

and He will answer. Even if the person is not a believer or is skeptical, you can still pray for them

and oftentimes, we are called to do just that.

Yes, sometimes it can take many times praying (or even years sometimes) to pray for someone or

for a situation to change. Continue to pray for them because you very well could be saving their

life and one day, they may just thank you for it!

~ 9 ~

IF GOD IS MAKING YOU WAIT, EXPECT MORE THAN YOU ASKED FOR

Just as the title of this chapter suggests, if God is making you wait for something, be prepared to receive more than you asked for. God is a respecter of people and of time, so He knows how hard it can be when you need to wait for a prayer to be answered. As such, when He makes you wait, know that He is preparing more for you than you even asked for.

Here are some examples of this concept in application:

- When Angie prayed for a new job and she waited 3 years to get the position of her dreams, she instead got called into her boss' office and was offered a position 3 levels above what she had even asked for. That is God showing up!
- When Daniel asked for a new kidney for his son, and the hospital said one wouldn't be available for years, Daniel dug in deeply to pray extra for his son. No kidney had yet become available but the doctors said Daniel's own

kidneys (which they thought had already shut down) continued to work for 5 years, just long enough for the new kidney to become available and the transplant to be successful. That is God showing up!
- Roula asked for God to rid her of the persistent feelings of depression. She was tired of crying, of taking antidepressants and of feeling a total lack of energy. God brought a wonderful pastor into Roula's life who was able to talk to her about the issues she had been experiencing. Roula explained that she had prayed for so long for the feelings of depression to leave her but they simply weren't. Roula and the pastor prayed deeply for Roula to feel better. Slowly, she began to find her sense of self. It may have taken Roula 4 years for all of those bad feelings to go away but they did and now, Roula is a nurse helping others feel better each day. That is God showing up!
- Mariann was praying for her daughter to be released from the sex trafficking ring she had gotten caught up with. She had been abducted from school from her supposed boyfriend and was being forced to work as a sex worker. Mariann prayed for 4 years for her daughter to be released and for her to find her way home. One day, as she was buying groceries, she got a call from an agency that rescues trafficked women and they said that they had found her daughter and that they were going to raid the home she and other trafficked girls were enslaved in. It took 4 long years but Mariann's daughter was released and amazingly, Mariann's prayers that not one hair on her daughter's head be touched was answered. Her daughter (after being released) explained to her mom that due to circumstances she didn't even understand, that she never happened to

be called to serve. In fact, each time her "turn" came up, she got passed over. Mariann had her daughter back and so did many parents and guardians, all of whom escaped and found their lives since being trafficked. That is God showing up!

- Cristina had been looking for and praying for her husband. She waited 2 long years for him but not only did God bring her her husband, but He also brought her a husband for her sister, who happened to be her husband's best friend. All 4 ended up being the best of friends and living their lives together. That is God showing up!
- When Geraldine lost her passport in a foreign country and needed some help getting back home, she didn't know who to turn to. She was in a foreign country and didn't speak the language. She was also limited on money so she was worried about how she was going to make the money she brought with her last. She prayed for God to help. 1 day later, as she was sitting and waiting in the train station, along came Paulo. Paulo lived in the country but also spoke fluent English. He was good and kind and helped her each step of the way, even going to the local passport office to help her papers get sorted out again. He offered to pay for a hotel room so she would have a comfortable place to sleep so that she was able to handle the following day's travel. Not only did Geraldine get her papers sorted out, but she also met Paulo, a wonderful man whom she ended up dating and marrying. That is God showing up!

Leaning on God

I want to emphasize for you, dear reader, the importance of leaning on God for prayers, for help, for salvation, for all areas of life. Life can and will get complicated. Jesus Himself said (John 16:33) *"I have told you these things, so that in me you may have peace. In this world you will have trouble. But take heart! I have overcome the world."* This is God letting us know that He sees and knows that we will have difficulties in this world but that He has overcome the world and that He knows that He can help us. That means that whatever we are going through today, He is there, ready, and available to help us through everything and anything. Nothing you are going through is a surprise to Him and it is important for you to know that He is going to bring you through any difficulty....if you ask Him to.

In other words, we were never meant to "do life" on our own. There is a reason we are called "sheep" and "flock". Sheep need to be protected from the wolf that lingers. That wolf can and will look different from person to person - the point is that the wolf is going to be something or someone that is posing a problem and a challenge for you, your friends, your family, loved ones, etc. As such, we need to stay close to the Shepherd.

As the title of this chapter indicates, if He is making you wait a while for your prayer to manifest, it is because He is going to bring you more than what you have asked for. He is going to bring you greater in an effort to let you know that 1) He is there and He is listening 2) He is in your corner 3) He is honoring the time you have put into praying 4) He is honoring your faith

When we pray, God goes to work immediately, moving things and shifting things in our favor. He does this for every person who takes the time to pray. This is God honoring our prayers and our faith.

It takes courage to bring a problem to God. It takes courage to say that "I don't have to deal with this on my own. I am going to lean on God and get His help through it." When we do this, God immediately goes to work on our behalf and does so in ways you will likely not be able to see immediately.

What have you been "doing" on your own and for which you recognize that it may be time to include Him? Reflect using the space below.

ANOTHER GREAT BOOK BY AWARD-WINNING AUTHOR, DR. CHRISTINE TOPJIAN

~ 10 ~

THE POWER OF ONE & THE POWER OF SOLIDARITY

When I was starting my own walk with God, I didn't have anyone with whom I felt I could pray. I wasn't even sure of what I was doing and I was certainly not sure of those around me - if they wanted to pray, if they could, could I trust them with the info of my prayers, etc.

I really quickly and soon learned by beginning to read up from Christian ministers and preachers (thankfully!) that we do not have to have anyone else to pray with. God hears the prayers of every single person and honors every prayer you make. In other words, I didn't then (nor do I now need) and neither do you need and have to pray with someone else. You could be alone and you could not have someone with whom to pray. Pray anyway. God hears it, will acknowledge it, will count it for you and will get to work immediately. This is what I mean by the power of one! You are one person and you are so valuable to God - He will hear and He will answer your prayer.

If you want to pray with others, this can work too and this is what I refer to as the power of solidarity. When we pray with others, God hears and honors those prayers too. He listens intently to what we say with our mouth or with our heart, and He respects that we are taking the time to pray for someone else too. This is why many groups, organizations, and churches do choose to pray together. There is great power in praying together and we have to remember that praying with others can often bring people great comfort, great joy and a feeling of solidarity and belonging. My point is just that you can pray on your own (and that is effective) and you can pray with others (also effective). Either way, your prayers are heard and honored by God.

Prayer Is A Two Way Conversation

This is one of the most important points I can make in this book and I have mentioned it in my other books as well but it is so important that it bears repeating: prayer is a 2-way conversation, which means that we must must must also listen to what the Holy Spirit wants to say to us about our prayer. Yes, the Holy Spirit still speaks to people today.

I have come across people who had told me that they did not want to pray because someone had told them that either 1) God no longer listens to or answers prayers 2) That God isn't interested in their life so what's the point in praying.

Both totally untrue and very detrimental to the life of the person. When any person takes the power of prayer away from us, they are truly doing us a disservice and they are taking away our power. Let's not let anyone do that to us.

God answers prayers today and He is interested in every aspect of your life.

God answers prayers today and He is extremely interested in every aspect of your life. He was interested in every aspect of your life from the time before you were even born to today and until your last breath and beyond. In Luke 12:7, it is written *"Indeed, the very hairs of your head are all numbered. Don't be afraid; you are worth more than many sparrows."* This gives you an idea of how valuable you are to God - He has counted every hair on your head and cares deeply about every tiny, minute, and microscopic detail of your life! Talk to Him about every problem you have. Pour it all out to Him, whether it's 2 am or 2 pm, He is ready, available, willing and there.

"What If It Doesn't Feel Like That"?

This is a question I have been asked and I felt this would be a good time in the book to address it and I hope to answer this question/emotion with care and sensitivity. Something that each person should know about the personality of God is that He is really good at all times and His love for you is immeasurable. He loves you that much and He desires to have a very close bond and relationship with you. Yes, terrible things are happening in the world but we have to keep in mind that man has free will and sometimes people make decisions that are completely contrary to God's will. As such, terrible things can and do happen every day. Does that mean that God isn't good? No, it doesn't. It means that man has free will and sometimes does not make good decisions and those decisions will negatively affect others. We cannot blame God for things being terrible in the world when He has asked people not to engage in terrible acts and they do anyway.

Fact is, God loves each person and wants us to do good unto one another. When we do that, wonderful domino effects happen. When we don't do that, terrible domino effects happen.

What will you choose to do? Use the space provided for your response.

~ 11 ~

PRAYING ACCORDING TO GOD'S WILL

When we pray according to God's will, what we are doing is getting into agreement with God and we are setting forth a motion of asking God to do what He wants for us. Of course, He doesn't need us to be in agreement with Him to bring about His will for us, but it is very helpful because this indicates to Him that you trust Him enough to pray for the very things He is indicating to you to have.

It is also really important to ensure that we pray in Jesus' name. Why is that? Because when we pray in Jesus' name, we are praying in the name of the most powerful name in the world. As such, our prayers are much more powerful.

For example, say you are wanting to marry person X but God is indicating to you that His will is for you to marry person Y. If we look carefully at the situation and we ask God to show us why He is guiding us to this person and not that, He will reveal His reasons to us and He will show us why He is guiding us to person Y. Revealing this means that He is going to show us things about person X that will bring to light truths that we may not have been consciously looking at. It means that when He shows us truths about person Y, He is going to show us why this person is the right one, over the other.

Let's not forget that God is all-knowing. He knows everything about everyone and He knows the heart of each person. He knows you and I so intimately well because He created us and He knows exactly what will be fitting for us and what won't. As such, we need to remember and respect that His perspective is the right one and the most insightful one.

I recall a woman who came to me in ministry on a few occasions said she felt compelled to marry a man named Joseph. She also mentioned to me that a Christian counselor had advised her that that man was not the right person for her but that instead, Mark was the right person for her. She couldn't understand why because she had been dating Joseph for many years and she felt she knew him very well and that he was a very good man. I pointed out to her that a prospective being a good man is not what is going to qualify him to be her husband and that she should be trusting God to lead her to and to show her why Mark is the right person. She went away and began praying about Mark and why he was the right person for her. She took several weeks before she returned and she said *"I feel like God is speaking to me so clearly and has told me repeatedly that Mark is the right person. Also, Mark has been withdrawing from me a lot lately and hasn't been wanting to come and see me for our regular date nights. Something definitely feels off."* I advised her to continue probing and asking God why He was guiding her from this man. She continued to do so and I promised that I would pray for her and with her as well. It soon became evident that over the years, Joseph had been lying to her about several aspects of his life and had been much less than honest with her. He had been misleading her and this caused her much grief and pain. She had trusted him so completely and to face the realization that he had not been truthful was a great burden. I then advised her to pray through the pain and for her to ask God to help her through all that she was going through. Into her life came a friend from her past with whom she had been wanting to reconnect. This old friend was returning to her life at the perfect and opportune moment - she remembered the many long conversations they had had and how she had been such a supportive friend to her. This lady felt really grateful that God had answered her every prayer and had guided her to His best for her - not to what she thought was best for her.

One of the Wisest Things We Can Do

Reader, one of the wisest things we can do is to ask God what His will is for us. We can ask Him to be very specific and precise and we can ask Him what He wants us to see, feel, acknowledge. It is amazing that when we begin to understand and tap into what His will for us is (as opposed to what our own will for us is) we can begin to see why He is guiding us to this and not that and how He has given us the tools, skills, resources and abilities to do those things. God never leads us to do something unless He has given us the tools to do it. He is a God who sets us up for success, not failure.

Suggested prayers for understanding God's will:

Lord Jesus, I am asking You to come into my heart and to speak to me about Your will for my life. Speak to me so clearly that understanding Your will will be unmistakable for me. I thank You in advance for answering my prayer. In Jesus' name. Amen

Jesus, I feel confused about the direction of my life. I feel that I am good at _____, _____ and _____ but I am unsure of where You want me to be and what You want me to do with my gifts. I am asking You to speak to my heart and to show me Your will, ways and direction. In Jesus' name. Amen

Holy Spirit, I come to You today asking for Your help, Your wisdom and Your insight for my life. I would like to ask You to help me know and move in the direction(s) of Your will for my life. I would like to ask You to help me do Your will by opening the right doors and closing the wrong ones. I will step into the doors You open. In Jesus' name. Amen

Father God, I feel unsure and confused. I am not sure amongst all the things vying for my attention in this world where I am supposed to be going and what I am supposed to be doing. As such, I am asking You to make my path straight and show me where You want me to go, when and how. I know that You are a God that answers prayers and makes Your will known. I am asking You to do that for me today and to make the path straight and clear. In Jesus' name. Amen

Be and Remain in Faith & in Gratitude

One of the most important aspects of our walk with God and to Him fulfilling and causing the manifestation of your dreams, goals and desires is to thank Him for having already fulfilled and answered your prayers. When we thank God ahead of time, that is us telling Him that we are so sure of His goodness and that He will answer and will deliver the manifestation of our prayers. In other words, it tells us that we are:

- So sure of His abilities that we are already thanking Him for blessing us
- So sure that He will do for us what is good that we are thanking Him ahead of time for helping us out

- So grateful that He is God in our lives and so we are thanking Him for being so good to us
- We are solidifying our faith and telling Him that we are grateful and glad that we stayed or are staying in faith while He works at answering our prayers and bringing us His best for us
- Shows others that your faith is strong and that if you are trusting in God before the fulfillment of the request, that maybe they too can trust Him with their dreams, goals and desires

Others Watching Us & Getting Influenced

Remember that people around us are always watching, looking, learning and observing. They are always looking and observing to see what others are doing and how they are doing it, in addition to whether our prayers are getting answered. This is part of human nature and doesn't really ever stop. We are even taught in our schools to look around and see what others are doing and how they are conducting themselves, and we are always encouraging people to be mindfully good. As such, we are in the habit of looking to see what others are doing, observing (sometimes quietly) and taking in the actions and behaviors of others. When we stay in faith, thank God, pray, go to church and show that we are leaning on and relying on God, we are silently and quietly influencing others to do the same. They are looking to see how your dreams, goals and desires are being fulfilled because, very simply, they too have goals and desires that they want to see fulfilled too. They are looking to see if things work out for you and if something is taking time, how you will react to the time it is taking. That transit time is really important because that can often be the toughest part of the waiting in faith and others will be watching and waiting to see how you will handle that time.

I recall very vividly how a friend of mine who is not a Christian decided that she would begin praying because as she put it, "I know you and see you and trust you, Christine. If you're doing it, I trust that there is something to it." That was a very high compliment for me, one that I have never forgotten and while of course I am not perfect, it was life-affirming for me to receive such a note of high worth from her. I feel that it is important that when we are leaders, that we do our very best to positively and strategically follow God's lead and demonstrate His love for others, to others. When we are mindful about our words, our actions and our steps in a Christian life, we are providing a good, solid example to others about our walk and how we are relying on Jesus to guide us with His infinite knowledge.

Another example I remember is when I had prayed deeply for something and was in transit time - I was waiting for the prayer to be fulfilled and I admit that I was trying to be patient but it was hard. This same friend (from the previous example) told me that she felt that it was a long wait time and was wondering if I was going to keep waiting. I told her that I was going to keep waiting because this was not the first time something was taking time and was in transit in my life - this had happened before and I knew that when God makes you wait for something, He has even more up His sleeve and will bring you more than what you even asked for.

> The transit time can be difficult but remember that we can always ask God if He would give us the strength, the wisdom and the patience to keep holding on, to keep waiting.

The transit time can be difficult but remember that we can always ask God if He would give us the strength, the wisdom and the patience to keep holding on, to keep waiting. During the transition time, I often like to think of the amazing sense of accomplishment and how pleased I will be when the manifestation of my prayer happens and I have gotten what I prayed for. It's the same as when we do something that is meaningful but hard (maybe like working out intensely by running on the treadmill) - we know how hard it can be to keep going on the treadmill and even though we are panting and sweating, we know that we are doing lots of good for our minds and bodies, and that we will be really pleased with the hard-fought battle.

~ 12 ~

TAKING ACTION ACCORDING TO GOD'S WILL

Our actions taken to reach our destination are also tremendously important and we need to pray to know what God guides us to what strategic actions need to be taken.

How do we know what strategic actions we have to take?

Simple. Pray to know. Pray for God to speak to your heart and to tell you what actions need to be taken. This is part of faith.

I will explain further: prayer (as I said before) was always meant to be a two-way conversation, in that you speak to God and He speaks back to you. He will answer you and unfortunately, this is a piece of the equation that many people miss out on. They think that they just speak and that's it. They forget to get the volley back.

God speaks to us in many different ways. He can speak to you via another person and He can speak to you directly. For some people who may not be tuned-in or listening, He may try to reach you through other people. I know a few friends and acquaintances I have that regularly ask me to check-in on something for them so that they know how they are supposed to proceed.

Here are some examples of questions asked and guidance given to the person asking, seeking and praying for it. You may notice that the format is questions and answers - this is what many refer to as journal format.

Person: God, I'd like to know how to help my kid. He seems to not know which way to go or what he is doing. Please help.

Holy Spirit: Your son is angry inside and needs an outlet to help him deal with his anger. As his mother, you need to spend quality quiet time with him so that he can let you in on what he is feeling and what happened that made him feel that way. Without doing that, your son will continue to get angrier and angrier and will continue going more wayward.

Person: Will he open up to me, though? I've asked him before but got nothing from him.

Holy Spirit: You previously asked him in front of other people. He will never respond to you that way because the issues are private. Speak to him privately, respecting his need to keep the information private and personal, between you and him. He will open up to you because he loves you. You are his mother and frankly, he has been waiting for you to ask him. He doesn't want to feel this way. He wants to feel happy and good about him and those feelings won't happen until he has an opportunity to let out what is bothering him and to have you all deal with everything.

Person: Thank You, God, for this insight and revelation. Is there anything else I need to know or do?

Holy Spirit: Yes. Continue checking-in with Me, asking Me questions, probing and asking me more. It is only via asking probing questions that I will be able to reveal to you what is needed and how to proceed. I love that you are asking Me questions. Continue, child. Good.

Person: Thank You, Lord!

Person: God, I feel angry with You. I've been going through so many issues in my life and in my marriage. I feel like everything is falling apart and I don't know how to fix any of it! Please help!

Holy Spirit: Daughter, I am here. I am here to help you. The reason you are going through such trials is because you are never asking Me what the right path is for your life. You married a man without asking Me who he was, what were his true intentions, and you had a child with him at a time when he was not being good, kind or faithful to you. This man you married was never from Me nor was he intended to be your husband. You made that decision on your own, without asking Me or consulting Me or your church elders, who are good and honest people and would have told you and shown you much about this man whom you have built your life around.

The time has come for you to stop looking to this man for love, validation and goodness. He will simply not bring that to you because he is, in every way, wrong for you. Your daughter is a blessing and she will grow up to love her mama and her papa but there are a few things you need to do regarding your marriage and the current state it is in. I ask you to spend time with Me, quiet time with Me in learning about Me, My goodness, My love for you and My will for your life. I can promise you that I will lead you to great depths of happiness and will guide you to what I always intended for your life. Will you do that, daughter?

Person: Thank You, Father. Thank You. Yes.

Person: God, I cannot stop drinking. When I stop drinking, I feel like the world is caving in and I cannot breathe. I feel like I cannot breathe and that everything around me is crumbling. I only feel good when I drink but it is ruining my life, it has ruined my marriage and I am never there for my own kid. My father, according to my mother, was also a mean drunk and would hit her. I don't want to be like my dad. Please help me!

Holy Spirit: Son, I am here for you. I will always help you and you have done the right thing in coming to Me. No matter what time it is, coming to Me is always the right move. I can and will help you. I will guide you to a very good sober living program and with the right prayers, with the right approach, your cravings for a drink will cease. You will stop wanting them. Your dad loved you very much but did not know how to show you that. He had no idea how to love in the ways that were needed and he did not know how to love your mom in the ways that she required. I will guide you to the sober living facility, will guide you to get help, and I will put a strength and a will power in your bones that you have never experienced before. You will kick this habit, that I can tell you. I will also guide you to the right person who will perform deliverance for you. You will get better, son, I guarantee it. And you did the right thing in coming to Me.

Reader, no matter what you are going through, no matter where in the world you are, no matter how much money you have in your pocket, the color of your skin or anything else, the

Lord loves you beyond measure and will always help you, will always be there for you. All you have to do is ask in prayer.

If you have never prayed before, that is not an issue. God still hears all prayers and He can bring you to the proverbial promised-land, no matter what or where that promised land is for you.

Inner Locution

Always remember, reader, that God speaks to us today as clearly as He spoke back in Biblical times.

(Matthew 28:20) I Will Be with You Always Even Unto the End of the World.

When God promised in the book of Matthew that He would always be with us, He meant that, and that means that He is always there, ready and willing to:

- Guide you
- Speak truth to you
- Reveal what is really happening in any situation
- Help you
- Open doors for you
- Bring you the help you need

- Give you the love that you need
- Reassure you
- Comfort you
- Provide a way when you don't see a way

I remember the context of a man I know whom I will call Tom. Tom was unfortunately suffering from very low self-esteem and was addicted to some very heavy illegal drugs. Tom had a loving family but he couldn't bring himself to get on the wagon and stay on the wagon. He was unwilling to commit to rehab or to AA meetings. His Christian sister and her Christian husband began praying for him. They prayed many times and very deeply that Tom would go to rehab and that he would stay for the entire course of treatment. Tom didn't have the funds for the rehab stay so his sister and her husband paid for the stay. Just prior to going, Tom confessed that going to rehab scared him very much and made him feel like a total loser. He explained to both of them that he was very worried about failing at yet another thing in life. His sister and her husband explained to Tom that going was the best thing for him and that rehab in no way made him a loser. In fact, going made him a stronger person who can admit that he needed some help and that was an awesome thing!

His sister and her husband asked their church to pray for Tom to go and to stay in rehab, getting the full treatment and all the help that he needed. They asked everyone in the church to pray fervently and deeply, asking God to work supernaturally in Tom's life. It took the transit time of 3 months to finally relent and to say that he would go and attend the rehab program and that he would commit to doing all the exercises and the soul-searching that was needed for his stay. Tom not only went to rehab but he stayed in the program and today, he works at the rehab center, helping others get sober. Tom always says how grateful he is for the rehab support, and to his sister and her husband for all the support given. He continues to be on the wagon and prays each day for the strength, the support and the ability to stay on the wagon.

Is there anything you sense you must take action on? Anything the Lord is guiding you to move forward on? Reflect in the space provided below.

100 ~ ANOTHER GREAT BOOK BY AWARD-WINNING AUTHOR, DR. CHRISTINE TOPJIAN

~ 13 ~

INTERCESSION

You may be asking yourself: *"What is intercession, Christine?"*

Intercession is when someone or a group of people pray for you because a) they feel you could use it b) you have talked to them about your issue(s) or matter(s) and they feel they may be able to help you c) they are trying to do something nice in supporting you d) you may have asked them to

When a person or when people intercede, it means that they care about you and they want to see good things happen to you. As such, when they pray on your behalf, they have the opportunity to ask or request things from God that will help you. Again, they could be doing this because they felt compelled to help you or because you may have asked them to. Either way, this counts as prayers for you and in your good favor so if someone is interceding, they are doing something really nice and really good for you.

You may be having a really good day and all feels like it is going really well. This could very well be due to intercession

- someone may have prayed for you and maybe asked God to make your day better or brighter, for all things to work out well for you, or for God's protection to be on you as you go through your day. Either way, it's a really kind thing for them to do.

When people intercede, they are praying for things for you that will bring you happiness, good fortune, good tidings and more. What they are doing is petitioning for good to come to you. Anyone can do this for anyone else.

Now, some people may not be believers or may not be comfortable with you or with others praying for them for a myriad of reasons. It would be helpful for you to ask the person *"May I pray for you?"* and see what they say. One reason people may not respond favorably to this could also be because they don't know what you will pray. For example, I was praying with someone once and he was making the prayer for a particular marriage relationship to work out well. Now, I knew that that was not God's will for that particular marriage and so I had to really gently tell the person that that may not be the best thing to pray in that situation. So, if you would like others to pray for you (which is generally considered to be a really nice and good thing), you may want to tell them what you wish the specific prayer should be.

Here is a look at how that conversation may go:

Person 1: Hi, I know you have been through a fair bit lately and I wanted to know if you would be ok with me praying for you in that situation?

Person 2: Sure, I could use the prayers.

Person 1: Great, is there anything specific that you would like me to pray in this regard?

Person 2: Definitely. Could I please ask you to pray that I get the best possible promotion that God wants me to have? I have been working in this company for many years and would like to receive a really good promotion that catapults me to higher levels.

Person 1: Sure, I will pray for just that.

Intercession When The Other Person Isn't A Believer

This is a question I get asked a fair bit: *"Can I pray for someone who isn't a believer?"*

I would have to say yes! A person not being a believer can happen for many reasons - one of which may be that they have never experienced the goodness of God before, they may not be very familiar with God or simply, they have not had opportunities to hear sermons, go to church, etc. I would encourage you to pray for them and help them get close to God, help them find salvation and help them see that God is a very kind, loving God.

I know many people who have prayed for others who were non-believers in the past and after years or months of praying for the person, the person had a divine encounter, a divine revelation or something of the like and they then found themselves to be in close relationship with God.

Years ago, when I was not a full Christian and I was not practicing, someone prayed deeply and consistently for me. She prayed for me without my knowing and with the full knowledge that I had no idea who Christ was. I was caught up in wrong teachings and wrong experiences and she later revealed to me how much and how hard she had prayed for me. While she was praying for me, she was also talking to me about Christ and while I wasn't open about what she was talking about, I was listening (despite not really wanting to) and after I left her company, I was still thinking about what she had said and what she was trying to get across to me. Well, her efforts paid off and worked!

Soon thereafter, I began spending time in the Bible, learning and understanding God's word, what He is really like, what He is really saying about everything and I was beginning to forge a real relationship with God. And this was all because someone

People may not be open to a close, personal and intimate relationship with Christ from the get-go but with your prayers and your help, they can be and I say this not for the purposes of manipulating anything or anyone, but for the purposes of helping them find salvation and find Christ. **It is the best gift (truly) that we can give to someone!**

Praying For God to Bring Someone Their Blessing

As part of intercessory prayer, you can pray for God to bring someone the manifestation of their prayer sooner. Here are two suggested prayers for this:

Lord, I am praying to You today to ask You to please help _____. Please bring _____ the manifestation of his or her prayer, helping them increase their faith in You. Reveal Yourself to them, Lord, in a deep and meaningful way. In Jesus' name.
Amen

Holy Spirit, please work in _____'s life. Help him or her to see and feel Your goodness and that You are there for them, no matter what they are going through. You see all and You know all so You know exactly what they need & when they need it. Please help them with this, Holy Spirit. I pray for this in the name of Jesus. Amen

Good on You Too

When we take the time to pray for someone, we are also doing a good thing and so we should be feeling good about ourselves. One's relationship with God is the most important one we will ever have and so when we pray for them, God sees this and counts it for our benefit too.

Prayer Circles

A prayer circle is a team that works to pray for the needs of others. Prayer circles can and do look different from group to group but they are all there to pray for each other so that everyone can have their chance to pray for their own things and to pray for the wishes, dreams, hopes and desires of others.

There is a fair amount of trust that needs to go into being part of a prayer circle. Why do I say that? Because you are praying out-loud about things that are important and meaningful to you and a prayer circle (in all its forms) needs to be a safe space for everyone to bring their prayer requests. Prayer circles are places where people share information about health, money, relationships and more - items that are usually considered sensitive for people. So if or when you are part of a prayer circle, please bear these things in mind. If a person in the prayer circle breaks one's trust, that could be something that is very damaging or even worse, irreparable in the eyes of the person whose prayer was shared with others outside the prayer circle and without their consent.

This happened to a lady I know who shared some very personal information about herself and some things she was struggling with and unbeknownst to her, someone in the prayer circle shared the information and she was rightly devastated.

She felt that the trust had been broken and the group moderator had to work overtime to re-establish the group's trust.

> Matthew 18:20 - For where two or three gather in my name, there am I with them.

What Does This Scripture Actually Mean

This Scripture means the following: God is with us always. We sometimes lose sight of that fact because we aren't able to see Him. But He is always with us and loves us and walks with us each day. When two or more are gathered, He is with them even more so. He walks with them, is available to guide them and often times, when those settings happen, the people in the group can actually feel the presence of God among them. It is really quite an extraordinary thing!

When God is with us, we can ask Him to do all of the following, all of which benefit us:

- Protect us from anything and everything
- Help us through something (even in that very moment)
- Give us ideas and wisdom that we need to successfully deal with something
- Carry us through when the weight of the burden becomes too great for us to bear

- Take something away that is hurting us or causing us pain
- Create a way to deal with something that seems impossible

Readers, one of the most touching intercessory prayers was when I heard a stepmother pray for her stepson. She saw that his drug and alcohol action was tearing the entire family apart and even though he had been to rehab on a number of occasions, it was not helping. Nothing seemed to be helping. So, this stepmom put that fact on the table and asked the prayer circle she had just become a member of to help her and to ask Jesus to deliver her stepson from this big problem. When she prayed, you could hear the hurt, hope and anguish in her voice. She was doing her best to keep it together during the prayer and at home, but as you may well suspect, that was not easy.

Nothing Is Impossible with God

I will talk about this more (because it is such an important point) in the next chapter but I want to really stress here that nothing (and I mean nothing) is impossible with God. He is capable of doing anything and everything. He stopped waves in the water and walked on water. All of Heaven and earth have been put under His authority so He is able to do literally anything. Even bend time because He Himself is timeless.

So when you feel like you are facing a huge, insurmountable problem, know that he is God and He can do anything. Let us not conform God to our idea of what He can do - let us conform to what the Bible says God can do, which is everything!

~ 14 ~

WORSHIPING GOD

There may be times where, during the transit time, people can get angry, frustrated or annoyed that the prayer request has not been answered fully enough or to their satisfaction and so they choose to turn away from God.

Their complaint may look something like : *"You are not working quickly enough for me, God, so I am going to do what I want to do."*

We have been given free will and so we can do whatever we want to do, separate from Him but that would not be wise. You see, God has ways that you and I don't and He works behind the scenes, setting you and others up for awesome success. So while it may seem that things are not moving quickly enough, it doesn't mean that things are actually not moving quickly enough.

This is where faith in who God is comes into play.

All of Heaven & Earth Are Under Jesus' Authority

Because of what Jesus did on the cross at Calvary, and His ensuing resurrection, we know that all of Heaven and earth are under His authority. This means that everything must obey Him and if it does not, there will be consequences.

As such, when you are facing a problem of any magnitude and you turn to Him for help, know that He is there, He can and will help you and that He is the perfect One in a position to help you. He has all of Heaven and earth at His command, even if things don't always want to admit that.

For example, in Mark 4:35 - 41, we see Jesus calming the storm by simply speaking to it. I don't know about you but I would have a bit of a harder time controlling something like a wave of water. Ultimately, everything is under His authority so everything has to comply with what He commands of it.

Now, we can see oftentimes that humans don't always follow this. Many humans do not consult with Him and sometimes, when others do, they are guided to do one thing but they end up doing another. They end up following the way that makes sense for them, as opposed to doing something that makes sense because God told them. My point is this: even if it doesn't make sense, follow through what God has told you to do. He controls everything so He would be in the best position to help you see something through.

The Fastest Way to Get A Prayer to Manifest

Simply put, the fastest way to get a prayer to manifest is by worshiping God. Letting Him know (through song, through words spoken out loud, through words spoken in your spirit, through writing it) that You worship Him and that You know He is capable and will move for your benefit. This is why many churches take the time to break out into song, showing God that they are worshiping Him and that they love and respect Him. This is what we need to do in a genuine and real way, to get our prayers manifested.

Another thing that is important here is that before you begin worshiping, cover yourself with His protection. Ask Him to protect you because darkness does not want you to worship God.

Always Working

> Psalm 121:4 Behold, He who keeps Israel
> Shall neither slumber nor sleep.

We have to recognize that when the Bible says that God is always working - it actually does mean that He is always working so He is working around the clock on your prayer request. You don't see the work being done behind the scenes so you can get angry, annoyed, or frustrated. Take heart and realize that

He is working to set things up for you so you need to trust in His timing.

Praying for understanding here - to know and understand how He is working behind the scenes for you would also be very helpful:

Lord, I prayed as You know and I am waiting for my miracle. I am waiting for my answered prayer. I know that You work behind the scenes and are setting things up that I cannot currently see. I would like to ask You to show me how you are setting things up, what all of that looks like and how I can be wise enough to spot the blessing when it is coming near. Please speak to my heart and my mind and show me these things. In Jesus' name. Amen

Having prayed this, wait and see what the communication will be. Wait and see what He will show you.

In order to remain patient while the prayer is in transit, you can pray this prayer:

Lord, I am asking You to give me patience while I am waiting for the prayer to come to fruition. I know that good things take time and that I need to wait. I am asking You to give me the patience that I need to wait for this prayer to be answered, and to show me how I can go and be a blessing to others while I am in waiting. In Jesus' name. Amen

Doing Good Unto Others While Waiting

One of the things that brings the most joy to the heart of God while you are waiting for your prayer to be answered and to manifest it to do good unto others while waiting. We are called to love our brothers and sisters and we are called to do good unto others. Imagine how much good you can do while waiting for your prayer and your blessing to be manifested.

Wouldn't it be wonderful to get your mind off of your own issues and troubles and to really work on being a blessing to someone else?

Take a few moments right now and jot down the names and situations of 2 people you can think of blessing while you are waiting. Make sure to use the last column to write down how you can help them and be a blessing in their lives:

Person I know	Their issue(s)	How I can help them/ How the Holy Spirit shows me I can help:

Being there for people is such a powerful act - one that is never forgotten. Think back to when you have done good and nice things for others. Even if they didn't respond the way you wanted them to or they did, know that you did a great thing for them. It could mean something simple or it could be something where you really went out of your way to help them. Either way, they should be very grateful for your help because helping someone out takes a great presence of mind.

Even just checking-in with the person can be such a big deal in their lives. They will feel loved, cared for, that you thought of them and that you were willing to do the act and to take the time to brighten their day. It can be as simple as sending a text message or a greeting card, calling them to see how they are doing or even sending them a little gift that has lots of meaning. Never underestimate how one such powerful act can be great and in return, how they can also one day help you.

A family member of mine is busy with a newborn but always takes the time to call or visit with her grandmother. Each day she calls her one time to check-in and to see how she is doing and then also visits her and brings her groceries once per week too. The grandmother always says how she feels cared for, seen and loved by her.

I remember one time when a good friend of mine had not messaged me in some time. I thought of her and began to send her texts of jokes and funny memes. She replied giggling but I noticed she was not writing back as she normally would. It was later revealed to me that while I was sending her funny texts and memes, she was experiencing a miscarriage. She told me later how much she appreciated the funny texts and thoughts because it got her mind off of the terrible thing she was experiencing. I had no idea that my texts were doing that much good for her but was really grateful to know that unbeknownst to me, they were helping her a great deal!

Readers, there are so many ways we can do good for others while we are waiting for our prayer to manifest and after our prayer has manifested. It is never wasted effort.

Let's take a moment and brainstorm this. Try to think carefully of people for whom you can do something good and positive. Try to think about past conversations you have had with them, past things they have said about their needs, wants and desires. Even if you can't help them accomplish a big need, you can do something to help them and that thing may free them up enough that they are able to carry through the time and the effort to complete their big need. For example, I once babysat for someone who needed to go to an interview. She didn't ask, I offered because I could see that while I couldn't get her the job she was seeking, I would be able to help free her up and free her mind of worry for the baby so that she could go and really deliver on that interview.

Take some time now and think about this by filling in the chart below:

Remember to ask the Holy Spirit to illumine your mind and to see what He wants to show you as well.

	Person I can do good for	Another person I can do good for	Another person I can do good for
What they might need			
What they might need			
What they might need			
What they might need			

Any additional thoughts and reflections you would like to add? Any journaling? Use the extra space provided here to write things out.

~ 15 ~

PRAYER MANIFESTED...PAY ATTENTION!

Sometimes, our prayer can be answered and has manifested but we were not paying attention, so we miss it. How do we miss it? Because it may not look like what you think it should look like.

I remember really clearly how a prayer of mine came to fruition after months and months of waiting but because it didn't look anything like what I thought it was going to, I did not pick up on it and totally missed it! Boy do I regret that!!

My point is this: pay attention. As soon as you get to praying, God gets to work, so you should know and keep it in mind that the manifestation of your prayer will be happening. You can (and should) also pray for wisdom to know what the manifestation of the prayer will look like. It may not look like you think it will but that is ok, you just need to be paying enough attention and clarify things with God and with the person or people involved.

For example, if I had asked the person in question "You are saying this and I am taking it as such, am I correct in how I am interpreting this?" then listen for their reply. You will need to pay close attention because they are explaining their meaning and their reasoning and it could very well be the answer you were seeking.

For example, I had interviewed for a position one time and I felt confident about my chances of getting the job. I waited the appropriate amount of time for them to formally offer me the position but instead of it having happened that way, the lady I interviewed with called me and revealed doubt that I would want the job. It sounded a bit like I had not been successful in my process and that she would not be offering it to me. I needed to clarify, so I asked "May I receive clarification that you are not offering me the position?" and she immediately replied "No, we want to offer it to you but we were wondering if you still wanted the position because you have a lot of experience in this area."

So, they were thinking that I was no longer interested in the job and I was thinking that they did not want to hire me. Had I not clarified her intended meaning, I could easily have lost out on the job. But I did clarify it and it turned out very well - I really enjoyed the position with that company and it was a great place to work!

"God, What Will It Look Like?"

God knows that misunderstandings can easily happen and that you can miss your prayer manifested. As such, it would be wise to ask Him, "God, what will the manifestation of the answered prayer look like?" or "God, show me please what this prayer answered will look like and what I need to pay attention to."

Truly, God loves it when we ask Him things. He is the good Father and He is happy when we show Him that we are relying on Him because we were made to rely on Him. He is the Shepherd. It is the Shepherd's job to show us the right way and to help us along the way while also protecting us.

We can also ask God for a vision or a visual of what something is supposed to look like. God regularly works with visions and visuals and they can give you a good idea of what things are supposed to look like. Now, I will also say that visions and visuals are not exact representations of what the real-life fulfillment will look like. They are a close depiction. This is part of how God works because it is basically Him giving you a hint and an idea of how things work but not the exact idea. He does this so that you can rely on Him more and ask Him more questions as the manifestation occurs (or what you may be thinking is the manifestation).

Use the space provided here to jot down your questions and any feelings, ideas, words, phrases, etc. that you get.

APPENDIX - THE POWER OF PRAYER

Prayers are powerful. When we pray, amazing miracles happen! Of course, most people would love to know that we can pray to reduce the transit time because God honors every prayer.

Here are some prayers you can pray to shorten the waiting time (the transit time):

> Lord, I am asking You to shorten the waiting time for the manifestation of the prayer I prayed to You earlier. You know which one I am referring to. In Jesus' name. Amen.

> God, I am coming to You in asking for Your help in shortening any waiting time and not allowing forces that may be trying to block or delay the answering and manifesting of my prayer. In Jesus' name. Amen

> God, please send Your angels to pray for me and to fight for me in granting me the physical manifestation of this prayer. In Jesus' name. Amen

> Holy Spirit, please shorten the waiting time to receive my blessing. Any forces or factors that are delaying things, eliminate them completely and bring me my blessing. In Jesus' name. Amen

> Father God, I trust in You. I trust in Your ways and I also ask You to cause the manifestation of my blessing without delay. In Jesus' name. Amen

> Jesus, please release Your angels and Your archangels to fight for me and for the manifestation on earth of my blessings. Please shorten the waiting time to the least amount of time possible. In Jesus' name. Amen

Father God, I thank You in advance for answering and bringing me my blessing. You have already done so much for me and I thank You for also bringing this to me. Please, Father God, shorten the waiting time and the "in-transit" time of this blessing too, so that I may experience with You the joy of this answered prayer. In Jesus' name. Amen

DON'T FORGET...GRATITUDE

Do you have a gratitude journal? A space in your phone where you write out your gratitude?

If you do, great! I would encourage you to use it and to write out daily all the things you are grateful for. Writing out your gratitude list helps you realize and contextualize the good things you already have in life. Recognizing these things and realizing that not everyone has these things is a grand thing.

We may often think that people have it better than we do, or that our blessings are "Ok, but..." What many fail to realize in that context is that God brought you those things and don't assume that someone else has them. Everything from the air in your lungs to your skills and talents are things you need to be very grateful for and use wisely because very frankly, how you use your gifts is going to dictate the kind of life you have. In other words, your gifts will dictate the quality of life you will have and if you have one gift or you have fifty, it's all in how you use it or them!

Take a moment now and write the following in your gratitude journal (or on your device or a piece of paper). Try to use something you will see again and again.

Now, your gratitude list will change as you progress in life but it is always worthwhile to look back and to see what you had put on your list and how your list changes over the years.

Try to make an entry that lists everything you are grateful for. Include your own skills and character/personality traits, include happy thoughts and joyful moments you have had, include the names of people who are in your life for whom you are also grateful and be sure to include past prayers you have prayed (for yourself and for others) that have been answered. I would argue that nothing helps us build faith like remembering answered prayers and remembering moments Jesus was there for you.

My Gratitude List

NOTES

This is a section you can use for all the notes you need to take. Jot down as you see fit.

Notes

ABOUT THE AUTHOR

Dr. Christine Topjian is a Doctor of Christian Ministry from Christian Leadership University, a Master & Bachelor in Education (both from Canisius College), a Bachelor of Commerce (from Ryerson University), and is currently working toward her second Doctorate in Divine Healing (from Christian Leadership University again). She loves writing books that help people become closer to God, Jesus and the Holy Spirit. Over the years, she has learned much and witnessed the power of God and how we can use that to our benefit and to bring about God's perfect will onto the earth!

Dr. Topjian runs her website at www.DrChristineTopjian.com and is regularly adding more news, information, features and a community to the site.

She runs a free (that is, no charge) Deliverance Ministry so if you are not sure what that is and you would like some info, please use the contact form on the site and reach out.

She lives and works in Toronto and is Armenian.

Blessings!